SPORTSMAN'S BEST

BOOK & DVD SERIES

FS Books:
Sportsman's Best: Inshore Fishing
Sportsman's Best: Offshore Fishing
Sportsman's Best: Snapper & Grouper
Sportsman's Best: Sailfish
Sportsman's Best: Trout
Sportsman's Best: Redfish
Sportsman's Best: Dolphin
Sportsman's Best: Snook
Sportsman's Best: Kayak Fishing
Sportsman's Best: Sight Fishing

Sport Fish of Florida
Sport Fish of the Gulf of Mexico
Sport Fish of the Atlantic
Sport Fish of Fresh Water
Sport Fish of the Pacific

Baits, Rigs & Tackle
Annual Fishing Planner
The Angler's Cookbook
Florida Sportsman Magazine

Florida Sportsman Fishing Charts
Lawsticks
Law Boatstickers
Field Guide
ID Lawsticks

Author, Mike Holliday
Edited by David Conway and Florida Sportsman staff
Graphic Design by Mark Naumovitz, Drew Wickstrom
Illustrations by Joe Suroviec
Copy Edited by Sam Hudson and Jeff Weakley
Photos by Sam Root, Pat Ford, David McCleaf, In-Fisherman magazine,
Ross Purnell at Fly Fisherman magazine and Florida Sportsman staff

First Printing
Copyright ©2012 by Florida Sportsman
2700 S. Kanner Hwy., Stuart, FL 34994
Printed in the United States of America

ISBN-13: 978-1-934622-51-3
ISBN-10: 1-934622-51-6

Find us on Facebook
twitter
www.floridasportsman.com

SIGHT
FISHING

CONTENTS

SB

SPORTSMAN'S BEST
SIGHT FISHING

Right Now

Modern life is a minefield of uncertainties: investing in the stock market, buying a new home or truck, deciding on healthcare options, politics, insurance. Shoot, buying a book can be daunting!

You make informed decisions as best you can, but there's no getting away from that sense of feeling your way blind.

Sight fishing, more than any other kind of fishing, returns to its practitioners a gratifying, elusive sense of control and instant feedback.

You can see a fish clearly. It's within your range. The moment you cast you know something is going to happen.

The fish will either take your lure . . . or not.

It's either this, or that, right now. No waiting for the shoe to drop. No excuses. You do your job, and success or failure is decided on the spot.

When you're merely casting toward a likely looking feature, say a rockpile or stump, you're submitting again to that cloud of uncertainties. It's not only a question as to whether you've selected the right lure or bait for the conditions, but is a fish even there at all? A sudden, unexpected strike conveys a gratifying thrill, but a fish-less morning leaves you with countless, annoying questions. It's all too familiar, the stuff of everyday existence.

Sportsman's Best: Sight Fishing will put you in the position to narrow things down. Author Mike Holliday is the ideal tour guide for diverse waterways, from his home surf in Southeast Florida, to the tropical bonefish flats, to midwest bass lakes, to the trout streams of the mountain West.

Holliday conveys valuable tips on tackle selection, reading the water, interpreting fish behavior, and calculating your approach. The photography and artwork have been carefully selected to show you ways to get closer to fish, to at once simplify and enhance your experience.

Okay, sight fishing will always have elements of suspense, as with all fishing. You never really know how a fish will react. And then there is the appreciation of a scene that strikes a chord deep within our souls. As we observe a wild fish make a critical, instinctive decision, we know we're watching something few persons will ever have a chance to see. It's entertainment rendered on a high-definition screen as big as the ocean.

But back to those uncertainties. Surely you're wondering, will I see a return on my investment in this book? Will I be forced to wait until the very end to judge its merits? Should I look elsewhere for guidance?

Turn the page . . . I think you'll enjoy it right away, like a tarpon crashing a well-placed fly.

Jeff Weakley, Editor, Florida Sportsman Magazine

In shallows, a wake is spotted, and the angler above tips off his friend. "Cast, 1 o'clock, now!"

Intent on the pursuit of a finning bonefish on a Biscayne Bay, Florida flat, anglers team up to sight fish.

Why Sight Fishing

Sight fishing, while one of the most rewarding angling techniques, is also one of the most difficult. It pits the angler's senses and skill set against everything a fish does to survive. Unlike other forms of fishing, where the angler is arbitrarily trying to encourage a fish to eat, with sight fishing the angler picks his target, approaches it stealthily, presents the offering and does whatever else it takes to get that fish to eat. And when that fish does eat, it's usually a fantastic bite.

From streams to rivers, lakes, bays and oceans many of the most sought-after gamefish in the world can be sight fished. That added element of difficulty and understanding of the fish you pursue makes catching it by sighting it even more special. Any angler can catch a fish, but sight fishing a gamefish is among the most rewarding styles of catching the fish you pursue.

In many ways, sight fishing is much like hunting. You spend time actually locating, identifying and stalking your quarry before you ever attempt to nab it. Each of these elements requires a specific skill set, one built on experience and knowledge of the fish you pursue. So as with hunting, firsthand experiences lead to a better understanding of your quarry's habits and idiosyncrasies, which in turn allow you to become more successful on the water.

The more you know about the fish you pursue, the better you become at locating them on a regular basis. Fish are also creatures of habit, so where you find them one day, you are likely to find them again under similar circumstances at that time of the year. With experience comes a better understanding of what to look for, where to look and how to look for the fish so that you can spot them long before they sense your presence.

One of the toughest parts of sight casting is learning to approach fish and get off a cast or repeated casts without being seen by that fish or other fish in the area. A lot has to do with the direction of approach and remaining in the fish's peripheral vision while reducing your own profile and restricting movements. It's an exciting game of cat-and-mouse, one that comes with a personal reward at the end when successful.

Unlike with most other fishing techniques, with sight casting you get to watch the fish react to your offering and eat it, and it produces some of the most memorable bites you'll experience as an angler. While most of the time you "feel" the strike, with sight fishing you not only "see" and "feel" the strike, but you direct the actions that lead to that strike by watching the presentation and reactions of the fish. It all leads to the epic attack of your offering by a gamefish, which becomes forever etched into your angling experiences. You just don't get that on a regular basis from other styles of fishing.

Sight fishing will always be one of the most rewarding fishing techniques, but it doesn't come easy. It requires skill, patience, knowledge and effort, which is why when you do everything right and overcome all the protective senses of the fish you're after and get it to eat, you will feel the personal reward that comes with an intimate understanding of the fish. That is the sport which brings so much enjoyment to our lives.

Mike Holliday, Author

CHAPTER 1

The Appeal of
Sight Fishing

Of all the different styles and aspects of fishing, the visual element is one of the most appealing and consistently rewarding. There's something inherently special about spotting a fish, making a good cast and giving enough action to your lure, bait or fly to get a reaction from that fish. That thrill of the visual element combined with the skill and knowledge of their quarry keeps sight fishermen returning again and again to the water.

Sight fishing requires effort, skill, knowledge and patience. You can't just arbitrarily make a cast and catch fish. There's a level of anticipation and several angles of approach that have to be worked out in your mind to be successful. That requires thought, exertion, practice and, at times, instinct.

It's you against the fish in the fish's realm—natural senses against your knowledge, experience and skill.

To "catch" the same fish twice at one time—unaware in its environment and on the hook—is sight fishing's challenge.

You have to become proficient at spotting fish, approaching those fish, knowing where to cast, estimating the angles and then making the cast count.

The Appeal

Fish are wild animals with a unique set of senses, acute and vastly different than the human senses. From hatchling to adult stages they are susceptible to predation, and hone their senses to avoid being captured. While fish may have better senses than humans do for the water, they don't have the analyti-

cal skills of the human brain, and that's where we have a distinct advantage over the fish we chase. We can outthink them.

While you can catch fish using simple methods, using your mind to catch a fish is even more fun! It's you against the fish, in the fish's realm—natural senses against your knowledge, experience and skill. When you use your mind to catch a fish, you experience the reward of good sport.

In the process, you'll also use all of your senses. With many types of fishing, you use your

senses sparingly to see the area you're wanting to cast to, to feel the twitching of the bait or the thump of the bite. With sight fishing, you see everything, often before you feel anything. It's an exponentially more visceral experience.

To be a successful sight fisherman, you need to master a variety of skills and know your quarry well. You have to become efficient at spotting fish, approaching those fish, knowing where the cast should go, estimating the angles and then making the cast count.

Comparison to Hunting

Sight fishing is much like hunting. As in hunting, there are a variety of techniques in sight fishing that can be used to pursue your quarry that result in success, and each one is different and requires a completely different set of skills. For instance, you can stake out your boat and wait for the fish to come by, much like a hunter would sit in a tree stand or blind and wait for a deer or turkey to cross his field of vision.

Both the sight fisherman and the hunter try to

position themselves in locations that are heavily traveled by their quarry. For the angler it might be along a point, dropoff, wreck or color change, while for the hunter it may be along a known game trail, food plot or natural tree formation that funnels the game in one direction. Whatever the scenario, both are trying to place themselves where they can see fish or game approaching and then react to that action.

Some cases require the angler simply to cast or the hunter to shoulder a firearm, while others dictate moving the boat for a better angle or circling downwind to avoid being scented. In all of these scenarios, the fisherman or hunter sees their quarry, reacts to its actions and makes snap judgments that affect the outcome. It's that skill set, that combination of experience, knowledge and effort that determine the success of the outcome, and the challenge of tricking a wild fish or animal in its natural environment is a big part of the appeal of sight fishing.

There's also the stalking scenario in sight casting fish and hunting, in which the angler or hunter actively moves in search of their quarry. Stalking requires patience and slow, deliberate movements as you try to approach within a certain distance of the fish or game you're after. All the while, the natural instincts of that animal are geared up to see your approach. But with that difficulty comes the reward and a sense of accomplishment that the sportsman also pursues.

So sight fishing and hunting have many similarities, and are very cerebral experiences. As you expand your knowledge of the movements and habits

There's also the stalking scenario in sight casting fish and in hunting, in which the angler or hunter actively moves in search of their quarry.

Tranquil moments followed by bursts of adrenaline pouring through your bloodstream—that's sight fishing.

Like a hunter in a stand, the angler sighted this permit near Key West from his perch on the casting platform and cage aboard his Chittum flats skiff.

of the species you pursue, and refine your stalking skills, you become more successful at intercepting and approaching your prey.

While the natural hunting/stalking relationship is an essential element of sight fishing, the overall appeal for many anglers is the visual aspect of the technique—seeing the fish, approaching it, feeding it and watching it eat. The sport of fishing really doesn't get better than that.

Visual Experience

Spotting fish requires knowledge of that species' habits and movements, and effort by the angler to be where they think the fish might be. Examples include looking for dolphin under a weedline, snook along a shoreline, bass bedding in the shallows or bluefish holding in a trough. For each species, there is a completely unique set of movements and skills required to find them.

Geographic location is another factor. Where

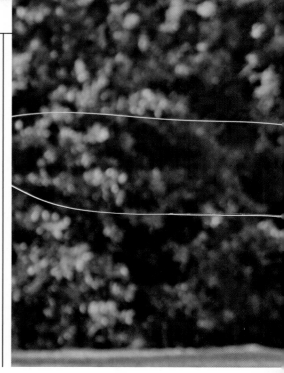

For each species pursued, like this snook, the angler must know his quarry's habits. Right, take any height advantage that you can to get the best view of the water when casting to fish.

It all comes together when the gills flare and your offering is gone. The overall appeal for many anglers is the visual aspect.

you find tarpon in the Florida Keys will be different than where you find them in the Everglades, or farther up the east or west coasts of the state. But once you do find the fish, the visual experience of approaching, targeting and getting the fish to bite is often the same. It's the same species wherever it may be found.

The components to the visual side of sight fishing include spotting the fish, watching its reactions as you maneuver closer for a cast, seeing the lure or bait in the water and the reaction of the fish to it, seeing the bite and the fish turn off, and then watching that fish

react when you sting it with steel. The entire time you are seeing the actions, reactions and posture of the fish—and sometimes many fish—and it all comes together when the gills flare and your offering is gone. It's the coolest moment in the sport.

There are so many actions, reactions and countereactions to sight fishing a single fish, that you'll soon find that you can't think your way through an approach. It becomes instinct to anticipate the direction and action of the bite. Every bite is unique, new and fantastic, which in part explains the enduring appeal of the game.

Knowing Your Quarry

There are times when a fish will eat without noticeable movement of its head or body, and conversely, times when it will simply explode on its meal. Fish will eat nonchalantly, excitedly, frenzied and with total disregard for their surroundings. And they'll also deny you for no ob-

vious reason. Unlocking the key to a fish's action is a big part of the key to successful sight fishing, and many times that comes from watching how the fish reacts to your offering and then reacting yourself by adjusting your presentation, bait, position or even all three. By knowing the response for each

There's only one way to learn—trial and error, so be prepared for the occasional letdown, and learn from the experience.

action on your part, you can avoid spooking or agitating the fish and concentrate on exciting and eliciting a bite.

Scouting out the classic scenario of a bass bed in shallows, left, to be followed by a protective bass blowing up an intruding bait, top.

As you learn the different nuances of each fish species, or how to interpret the scenario, you narrow your options for reaction to those that are pleasing to the fish. And there's only one way to learn—trial and error. Be prepared for the occasional letdown.

While you may be able to catch fish more effectively blind casting or working a general area you know fish are holding in, or in some cases by simply covering a lot of water, there is a feeling of accomplishment that comes with sight fishing that elevates the experience to another level. You'll feel the first thrill of that accomplishment when you watch that fish feed.

Watching the Bite

Watching a fish feed is a charge, even when you don't have a hook in what the fish is eating. Just seeing the fish in its natural element, relaxed and eating, enhances our sense of enjoyment of interacting with the marine world and our natural surroundings—two of the primary reasons most of us go fishing in the first place. Catching fish is just a bonus portion of the experience.

There are times when it pays to just stop and watch the fish. Watch them eat, move, react to their surroundings. It's a learning experience as much as it is a visually exciting one. Seeing the postures of the fish, what it reacts to (positively and negatively), how it moves, stalks and consumes its prey is an amazing moment in nature, and more importantly for fishermen, an education in a fish's feeding habits.

Whether you're watching a fish eat a bug, snatch a frog, grab a shrimp or engulf a baitfish, you're watching that fish in its natural element, and you're going to recreate that same bite at a later time. That bite is going to be infinitely more satisfying, because you are going to provoke it, and you are going to hook that fish, and you are going to watch it happen from start to finish.

As many different species of fish as there are, there are a similar number of bites and feeding styles. Some are dependent on the anatomy of the species—the way a sailfish stuns a bait by slapping it with its bill, then swims forward to engulf the stunned baitfish. Some fish are super aggressive and explode on their prey, like a peacock bass eating a fish off the surface or a snook blasting a mullet. Some pin their food to the bottom, while others cut it into pieces, and even others grab it in an acrobatic leap from the water. They're all different and fascinating to watch.

No matter the style of the bite, watching the fish change postures, react to the offering and then eat is one of the ultimate fishing experiences. Once you experience it firsthand and get that jazzy feeling of accomplishment, you absolutely have to have it again. And that is the appeal of sight fishing.

Now let's get started! SB

As clues go, this one of a tarpon lunging through a bait school is obvious, but close observation will yield volumes of info.

That bite is going to be more satisfying, because you are going to provoke it and hook that fish and you are going to watch it happen from start to finish.

CHAPTER 2

It's All About
the Eyes

One of the great pleasures of sight fishing is being immersed in the natural world flawlessly—so that not even your quarry is aware of your presence. How do you get into that world? Through the power and comprehension of your visual sense, which, when sight fishing, gets turned up to a greater degree than most of us use or need in daily life. For that reason, you'll want to do everything you can to protect and enhance your visual skills on the water to see things as you've never seen them before.

Even when a fish denies your offering you can learn something from it. Based on the concept that repeating the same action will bring the exact same result, you learn not to make the same mistakes. If you didn't see that denial, you're more apt to repeat that same action.

All eyes are not equal. Some anglers see better than others. Some are better at interpreting color and movement, shape and angle.

Fishing just off beaches depends heavily on seeing visual clues of fish— wakes, busting baits and feeding birds.

Find Your Target, Know its Path and Behavior

It's essential that you see the fish. You want to know at all times what that fish is doing, how it is reacting and whether or not it still might feed. When you make a cast, you want your bait to land in the best location to bring about a bite, but you have to know where the fish is to make that cast. If you can't see the fish, you can't lead it. Cast to one side or put

A shallow flat at low tide holds hints to where the fish will be at high tide if you see the colors and shapes that reveal them.

the bait right on its nose, and you often miss the bite because you've spooked the fish.

When you see a fish, you can gauge its movements, speed, direction and actions. You can figure out what it might do next, where it might go, how fast it will get there. When you know those scenarios, it's considerably easier to get your offering in front of it. Let's not forget that there's only one end of a fish that will produce a bite, and you want every cast you make to be to the correct end of the fish.

That being said, all eyes are not equal. Some anglers see better than others. Some are better at interpreting color and movement, shape and angle. Those are natural skills we're born with, although as you see more fish, you do acquire a better understanding of what you are looking for and what it looks like in the water, so you get better at spotting it. Try to spend as much time on the water as possible.

I know a fishing guide in the Florida Keys who's color blind. While not being able to differentiate between red and brown, he sees everything in black and white, dark or light. At times, it can be an advantage. For instance, when sight fishing bonefish, a species with a gray back and silver sides that often reflects the color of its environment, this guide sees the darker hues of the fish's back, and readily spots them before others because of his color blindness.

For the most part, you will use color as one of your visual clues to sighting fish as well as for spotting structure that may hold fish. Dark brown water inshore, for instance, usually points to a dropoff or deep pothole, while light brown water is indicative of water too shallow to hold most fish. Colors of objects underwater will also help you eliminate the items from consideration that have the shape of a fish but not the right color.

Color will also tell you the attitude of a fish. A billfish that has a flat black or copper color is tired or unenthused, while a billfish that turns a vibrant blue is "lit up" and ready to feed.

As you become more proficient at sight fishing you will utilize what you see to determine your course of actions, based on knowledge and experience. But you can't react to something or learn from what you can't see.

Importance of Quality Sunglasses

One of the key elements to good vision while on the water is a quality pair of polarized sunglasses. Polarized lenses cut glare, pick out areas of reflected and refracted light and often

Fishing was recently identified as the number one sport for eye injuries, so be sure to pay attention to the impact resistance of eyewear.

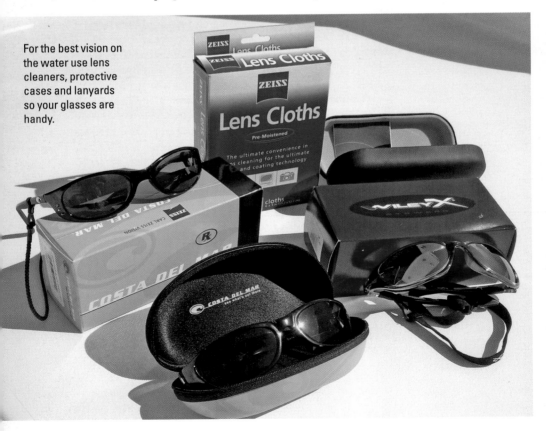

For the best vision on the water use lens cleaners, protective cases and lanyards so your glasses are handy.

Advantages of Polarization

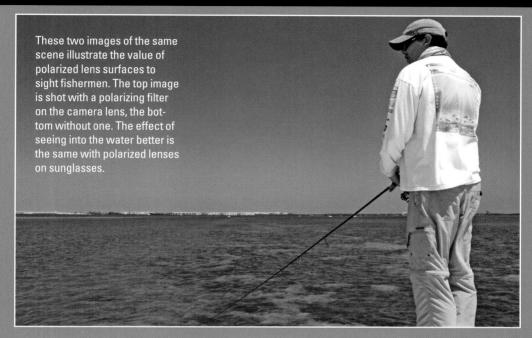

These two images of the same scene illustrate the value of polarized lens surfaces to sight fishermen. The top image is shot with a polarizing filter on the camera lens, the bottom without one. The effect of seeing into the water better is the same with polarized lenses on sunglasses.

Polarized glasses cut glare, pick out areas of reflected and refracted light and often accentuate colors, depending on the lens tint. They'll also allow you to look deeper into the water, which is super important.

What if the lure from the angler on the right side came flying back—head high—off a hooked fish?

nal tackle snaps back at the angler either from a stretched line or errant cast. Impact resistant lenses can deaden the blow and protect your eyes from permanent injuries. It's a good idea to keep your sunglasses on at all times, even during low light periods and rainy days.

One thing you want to remember is that not all sunglasses are alike. While a cheap pair of polarized sunglasses might cut through reflected light, they might not be protecting your eyes from UVA and UVB rays or have the right color to allow you maximum visibility. So in essence, they are fooling your eyes into thinking it's darker out and opening the pupils while exposing them to dangerous light that can cause permanent damage.

While not all sunglass lenses block all UVA and UVB light, a hat does. Wearing a hat with your sunglasses will block direct sunlight and protect your eyes from the direct rays of the sun, thus decreasing sunlight exposure to your eyes by as much as 80 percent. That still doesn't compare to the 100 percent UV light blockage that you'll get from a quality pair of sunglasses.

accentuate colors, depending on the lens tint. They'll also allow you to look deep into the water, something that's vitally important when pursuing fish that don't swim in shallow water or high in the water column.

Fishing was recently identified as the number one sport for eye injuries, surpassing basketball and handball, so while you're shopping for a quality pair of polarized lenses, be sure to pay attention to their impact resistance rating, as they might someday save your eyes.

The majority of eye injuries from fishing come when a lure, hook, weight or other part of the termi-

Choosing the Right Lenses

For those anglers who need corrective lenses, most of the quality sunglass manufacturers can produce their product with prescription lenses. While they can match the prescription for single vision, bifocal and progressive prescriptions, many of these prescription lenses are limited in their ability to curve and still maintain the

Maui Jim
Canoes

Maui Jim
Sailfish

Costa
Del Mar
Cheeca

integrity of the prescription. So when you start to look at purchasing prescription sunglasses you are often limited to specific styles.

In the long run, the advantages of quality sunglasses outweigh the costs. If you're going to spend much time outdoors, you should seriously consider investing in a good pair of quality sunglasses. There are a number of manufacturers producing quality lenses these days, with the prices dependent on the construction of the product. As a rule, the more you spend, the better glasses you get.

Glass lenses tend to be clearer and more scratch resistant than polycarbonate or plastic lenses. At the same time, glass is more likely to shatter, and thus offers less protection against flying sinkers or other projectiles. Superior optics or maximum protection? It's your call. Glass lenses are somewhat heavier, which may be irritating for some anglers to wear for long periods. You'll also find that composite materials in the frames will make sunglasses lighter or heavier, and more or less comfortable to wear. Like frame styles, the materials that go into the sunglasses you choose are a personal option, but there are some elements that you definitely want to keep consistent.

Lense Colors for Performance

Lens color determines to varying degrees how well you see into a specific color and clarity of water. Some lens colors perform best in dark water, while others excel in clear blue water. Choosing the correct sunglass lens for your style of fishing can have a big impact on what you see or don't see.

There are basically four lens colors of special interest to anglers: gray, amber, yellow, and copper or rose. Each lens color has a distinct application, and knowing this you can use your sunglasses to the best of their manufactured purpose. Some of

this is subjective, but in 40 years of fishing and in working closely with a major sunglasses manufacturer, I've identified general guidelines for color lens selection.

Gray lenses are the generally accepted standard for offshore or bluewater anglers because they maintain the color saturation and allow the wearer to see deep into the water column with a variety of blue hues. The ability to differentiate between colors deep into the water column is essential to spotting fish. The contrast of those colors will stand out because of the high saturation levels. For instance, the back of a wahoo will show brown against the blue field created by the water, while the sail portion of a sailfish will be a more vibrant blue than the darker blue field.

Amber lenses are the standard for inshore fishing in tannic or stained water, as well as most freshwater scenarios. Amber lenses bring out a lot of contrast, which is important when you're looking at things like different bottoms, rocks, grasses, trees or other structures. Any time you're bass fishing and look into the water, you'll see vegetation

Amber lenses bring out contrast and are popular for darker, stained inshore waters.

of different colors. While hydrilla might show as a darker hue of green, milfoil will be a brighter green with a tint of brown or red.

Amber lenses also pick up reflected and refracted light, allowing the angler to see shell beds on mud bottom or limestone along a grass flat. In stained water, amber lenses accentuate the color hues, allowing the wearer to see the different nuances to the colors that define what they are looking at, whether that be grass in shallow or deep water or sand along a dropoff.

Yellow lenses enhance colors and contrast to the extreme, allowing you to see deep into super clear water, as you'll find on the grassflats of the Florida Keys and many Caribbean countries. Often the water is so clear that light penetrates all the way to the bottom and colors wash out, so it's difficult to determine a light brown from a dark brown or light green. Yellow lenses allow you to see the colors better while really picking up the contrast between light and dark, which also makes these glasses excel in low light conditions.

Seeing colors on the flats is important for determining water depth and the bottom composition, but contrast will help you spot fish. Many of the premier flats species have colorations that mimic the bottom and help camouflage them from predators, but the contrast in colors will look like shadows. When you see a shadow move, you can track it until it takes the shape of a fish, then determine if you want to cast to it or not.

Copper or rose colored lenses enhance the color and contrast, and are probably the best all-around lenses for sight fishing because they accentuate the colors of everything from structure to fish, while providing enough contrast to see movement. They work exceptionally well in clear or stained water, and produce a combination of good color clarity and good contrast, so you see the bottom and marine life as well as the shadows of moving fish.

In the end, if you fish offshore, you're going to do well with the gray lenses, while inshore and freshwater anglers will do well with amber lenses, and flats fishermen like the yellow lenses. But for seeing objects and picking out movement, it's hard to beat copper or rose as the all-around sight fishing lens. At the same time, experienced anglers who rely more on pattern recognition may find lens color less important.

The thing to remember is that no lens does it all. Try to go with the lenses that best match the fishing you do the majority of the time, and even when the lens is not the top color for that type of fishing, a good polarized lens will dramatically improve your ability to see into the water and identify what you're looking at.

Some sunglass manufacturers also produce lenses with color mirror tints that may improve the ability of the angler to see fish and other objects. Those colors vary from purple to gold, silver, green and even blue.

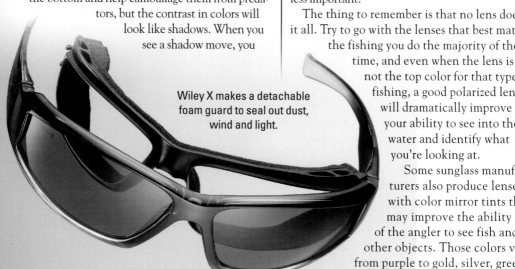

Wiley X makes a detachable foam guard to seal out dust, wind and light.

Gray lenses are popular for offshore use because they promote better vision of colors deeper into the blue water.

Blue mirrors match up well with gray lenses because they produce maximum contrast in bright water. They also excel in bright sunlight. The blue mirror serves to darken the gray and relax the eyes while increasing contrast when looking deep into the water. What you get is a pair of lenses that see deep into the open ocean water column.

When you're fishing in stained water, green mirror tints match up well with amber or yellow lenses because they provide contrast and enhance the color saturation. This is a good combination for fishing lakes, streams and inshore saltwater locations where the water is not crystal clear with a blue or green hue.

Silver, gold and purple mirrors enhance colors and maximize light transmission, so you see a lot more of the reflected light coming off of objects whether they're fish, rocks or other structure. In essence, they brighten colors to the extreme, and

let you see just about anything that moves. These mirror tints pair with all lens colors, but really make copper or rose colored lenses pop.

While sunglass frames are a personal (and often fashion) decision, keep in mind that the main function of the glasses is to help you see fish, not to make you look good. What you want to look for in sunglass frames are ones that fit tight to your face and don't let a lot of outside light in.

It's a common mistake to purchase sunglass frames that don't snug up tight to your face, allowing light in from the top, bottom or sides of the frames. Light getting in around the frames will cause your pupils to constrict and you to squint your eyes when looking toward the sun.

Many sunglass manufacturers now make frames designed to wrap around your face, holding the lenses tight to the eye socket and blocking out light. Frames with wide arms to block light from

ProTip: Sight Casting Bluewater Species

Any time you're sight casting fish offshore you want a quality pair of polarized sunglasses to help cut the glare on the water's surface and allow you to see deep into the water column. Most bluewater anglers prefer the photo gray lenses, which allow you to see colors well into the water column. One  of the big keys to sight fishing offshore is to cock your chin away from the sun direction to line up the polarization properly with the sun angle. It's amazing how that will open up your viewing depth into the water.

When sight casting migratory fish, you want to determine the direction the fish are moving, which helps you determine your angle of approach. In the Florida Panhandle, we get a big cobia migration in the spring, with the fish traveling from east to west. Knowing the direction of movement, if the fish spooks and goes down, it will typically resurface to the west of where you saw it last.

Scan the surface as you run, watching for irregularities in color and movement. Also watch for small fish—once you get used to spotting them, the big fish will really stand out.

You'll want to approach the fish from offshore facing toward the beach, and lead the fish with your cast, placing a live bait six to 10 feet in front of the fish. Cast a lure or fly 10 feet ahead of the fish and about 10 feet past the other side of the fish, so that the retrieve will take it directly into the fish's path.

When sight casting dolphin you want to look deep into the water column, not on the surface, the same with sailfish. Because you're in deep water there is no shadow, so you have to look for color that stands out, usually from the pectoral or tail fins or a flash of color from the fish's side. Be sure to look well around any floating weed, debris, structure or wrecks, as the fish like to sit five to 10 feet down around these items.

Also watch the posture and colorations of the fish. A sailfish that's shopping for a meal will be brown, gray or dull green, but a sail that's ready to feed will be a vibrant blue or black. Dolphin that have already been hooked or are spooky will often display stripes, while fish that are hot to eat will be bright yellow with green tails.

Captain Pat Dineen has lived and fished in the Destin area since 1975 and has fished extensively throughout Florida and the Bahamian Islands. After completing college and graduate school, he chose fishing as a career and established Flyliner Charters catering to sport fishermen.

Frigatebirds low on the water and seen at a distance are often the sign of a bite waiting to happen.

the sides are popular, too. There are also frames with small lenses on the sides to improve peripheral vision. At least one manufacturer—Wiley X—offers a soft foam "cavity seal" to block light as well as wind and dust.

Whichever style you choose, remember that when trying them on, wind and sun wreak havoc on your eyes and will not only tire them, but manifest headaches and other eye problems. You want to block out any light from the sides. With your eyes well-encased behind the sunglasses, they can relax and function at 100 percent.

Sunglass Accessories

Several sunglass manufacturers also produce plastic temple guards that slip on the arms of the sunglasses to block out light penetrating from the side. These are a quick fix if you find light entering from the sides and reflecting off the inside of the lenses, thus blocking your eyes from a clear look through the lenses. They simply slip on the arms, and can be manually positioned for the best light blockage.

There are other ways to limit light as well. Elastic face masks (Buffs, H.A.D.s, balaclavas by Simms, Columbia Freezer Wrap Headgear) have become popular among fishermen as a means of keeping sunlight off your face, neck and ears. When worn across the face, over the nose and cheeks, and pulled up high across the back of the head, these masks wrap around the outside of the sunglasses. They're effective at creating a dark zone on the sides of your glasses, making it easier to scan the water.

Hats for Blocking Light

While we're on the subject of hats, not all hats are created equal. Any time you're choosing a hat to wear when sight fishing you want to make sure it has a dark underside to the brim. Topside, a white or khaki colored hat will definitely keep your head cooler than a dark color hat because the lighter colors reflect much of the sunlight while the darker colors absorb them. At the same time, a light colored under-

side to the brim not only reflects light back into your glasses, but also creates a bright field or "wall" of white that inhibits your ability to see contrast.

The length of that brim also plays a factor when sight fishing, which is one of the reasons many fishing guides wear long-brimmed hats. The longer brim blocks out more sunlight, particularly early and late in the day when the sun is lower on the horizon. You can also tilt your brim or face downward in that same scenario, or if the sun is angled to one side, pull the brim down lower on that side to block the sun. You might look like a hip-hop angler, but you're also effectively putting the odds of seeing fish in your favor.

In a pinch, you can always shield your eyes from sunlight or block out the sun. Your hands make eye shields, and you can even cup them and position them tight against one side of your face on either side to block light. That simple act of shielding promotes better vision into the water. SB

Stu Apte, a reknowned and accomplished sight fisherman, uses glasses with side shields to block light.

CHAPTER 3

Tackle Options

I f you're going to dedicate the time to sight fishing gamefish, you want to skew the odds in your favor. One of the best ways to improve your ability to cast to, hook, fight and catch fish is to use the right gear. That means the gear that you know will be up to the task at hand and which you can use with confidence and accuracy.

As with any type of fishing, the right tools will make your life much easier and make your ability to catch fish more consistent. The fish have the edge when it comes to using their natural senses, but you have the edge when it comes to using your mind and those tools. With that in mind, let's look at the different types of gear that will improve your ability to sight cast fish.

One of the best ways to improve your ability to cast to, hook, fight and catch fish is to use the right gear. That means the gear that you know will be up to the task.

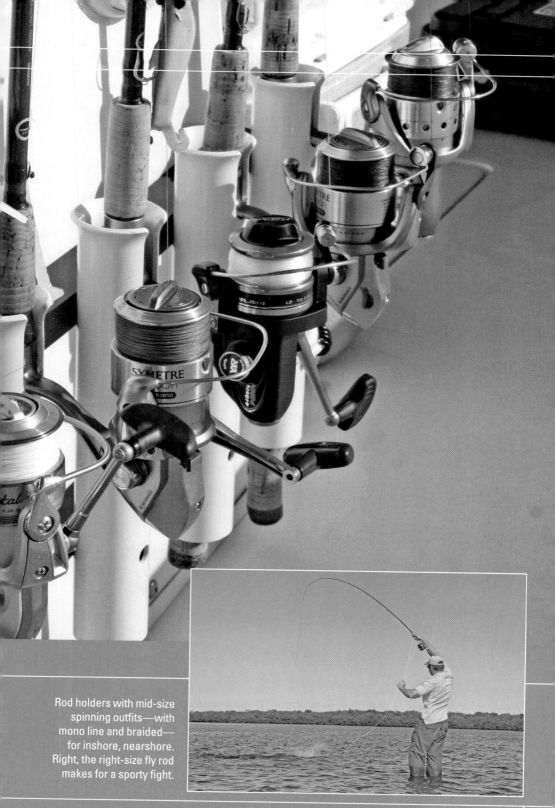

Rod holders with mid-size spinning outfits—with mono line and braided—for inshore, nearshore. Right, the right-size fly rod makes for a sporty fight.

Rods and Reels

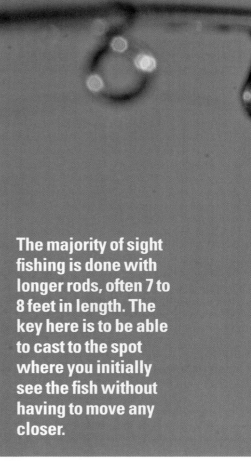

A general rule—though somewhat of a simplification—is that short rods cast more accurately, while longer rods yield more casting distance. With that in mind, you want to think about the type of fish you're after and the style of fishing you plan to do.

Because clear water improves your ability to spot and cast to fish, the odds favor you'll be doing most of your sight casting in moderate to very clear water which may or may not have a color tint. True, the clearer the water, the easier it is to see the fish, but it also makes it easier for the fish to see you. And if the fish you're after is in any way spooky or reacts to the angler's movement, then it's considerably more important to make a long cast than to put that cast on a dime.

Spinning outfits are the choice for casting big plugs distances nearshore and offshore.

The majority of sight fishing is done with longer rods, often 7 to 8 feet in length. The key here is to be able to cast to the spot where you initially see the fish without having to move any closer.

Given that train of thought, the majority of sight fishing is done with longer rods, often 7 to 8 feet in length. The key here is to be able to cast to the spot where you initially see the fish without having to move any closer, and a longer rod will usually make the difference between casting to a relaxed fish and casting to a fish that is on its guard.

For most bluewater applications, a 7- to 7½-foot rod is the best option, because it provides excellent casting distance yet allows an angler to throw a larger lure or bait. One thing you want to keep in mind is that the longer the rod, the greater the fulcrum created between the length of the rod and your arms when fighting fish. That means that longer rods are more difficult to fight big fish on. They create considerable pressure at the end of the rod and are harder to hold for long periods. That's why there are few applications for an 8-foot rod,

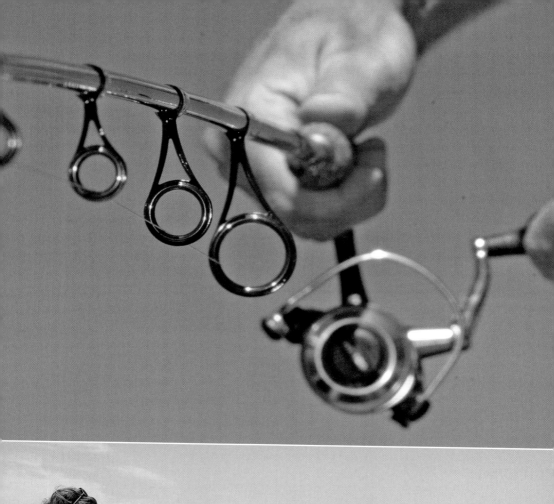

For most nearshore and offshore fishing, a 7- to 7½-foot rod provides good casting distance and fighting action for a variety of species.

Whether on baitcasting or spinning outfits, lures can be cast increased distances when polyethylene braided line is used.

cause there's no structure to hang on, the cast doesn't have to be super accurate to be successful. Often the angler is just trying to place a lure or bait past the fish or opening, and many times there are several fish in the area, so getting the lure or bait a long ways from the boat is more important than a pinpoint cast.

These longer rods also excel when casting small lures or baits because they add distance to a relatively light object. When paired with the superior casting distance of thin-diameter polyethylene braided line, the longer rod is often the last piece of the puzzle needed to make a super long cast to spooky fish in clear water.

when fishing in blue water. (Fly rods, which are almost always 8 feet or more, are treated separately at the end of this section.)

Freshwater anglers use a variety of rod lengths when sight casting, from 6 to 8 feet, depending on the scenario. When throwing to fish that are holding in small pockets in the grass or around visible structure like rocks or stumps, a 6-foot or 6½-foot rod is more applicable when using baitcasting gear, while a 7-foot rod is the choice with spinning gear. The shorter rod for baitcasting is simply more accurate when paired with a revolving spool reel.

Eight-foot rods are less commonly used in fresh water than in salt water, because anglers are rarely presented with the situation of super long casts to fish in clear water. However, there are applications for them. They are excellent for casting to schooling fish that are breaking the surface a long ways from the boat or beach. Any time there is the scenario where schooling fish are moving quickly and repeatedly coming to the surface, the 8-foot rod will give an angler the extra casting distance needed to regularly reach those fish.

Anglers fishing light tackle in inshore saltwater areas are the ones who most frequently go to the longest rods possible, and this is strictly to improve casting distance. In areas where the water is exceptionally clear, it's imperative that you make the longest cast possible. Fish moving along sandy shorelines, down beaches and around potholes are the most common scenario for long casts, and be-

Baitcasting Reels

As is the case when you're choosing the best rod for your specific fishing applications, selecting the reel to match the rod all depends on the technical side of what you are trying to accomplish. While spinning and baitcasting options are a personal choice, there are some distinct advantages to each.

Baitcasting reels come in two basic designs: the low profile reel that fits easily into the palm of your hand but has a limited line capacity; and the high profile reel that is considerably larger and thus holds more line on the spool. Line capacity should be one of the major factors to consider before purchasing a baitcasting reel. When targeting fish that don't make long runs, like bass and spotted seatrout, the low profile baitcasting reel is the best option because it's accurate, light and easy to master. When pursuing fish that often test the limitations of the tackle, like tarpon or sailfish, the high profile reels are the better choice.

You'll also want to look at the strength of the line you plan to fish, and that should determine what size reel you select. For example, if you're going to target bass in heavy cover with 50-pound braided line, use a larger low profile reel that can accommodate the thicker line diameter and has a drag system and gearing designed to handle that extra load. When fishing

Baitcasters were developed before spinning reels, and some anglers say that with a baitcaster's revolving spool they can cast farther and more accurately than with a spinning outfit.

lighter line for longer casts, the smaller sizes of low profile reels are applicable.

Any time you're looking at baitcasting reels, you want to consider the gear ratio of the reels. Gear ratio applies to the size of the internal gears and how much line they pick up with each turn of the reel handle. A baitcasting reel with a high gear ratio like 6:1 will bring in almost twice as much line with the turn of the handle as a baitcaster with a 3.2:1 gear ratio. That being said,

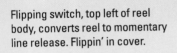

Flipping switch, top left of reel body, converts reel to momentary line release. Flippin' in cover.

Flippin' for Bass

Sometimes you have to dig through weeds to get to paydirt, and long ago bass tournament anglers developed techniques to get to fish under heavy cover.

Heavy flipping requires using a heavy sinker, up to 1½ ounces, to punch through thick surface cover like hydrilla or hydrilla mixed with other vegetation. Many bass fishermen use a 7½- to 8-foot heavy-action flipping rod spooled with at least 50-pound braid.

Lighter flipping around lighter vegetation, like hyacinths, duck weed or other calls for a 7½-foot medium-heavy or heavy action rod. Some anglers use 50-pound braid, while others go with 25- or 30-pound mono.

each reel has specific applications.

You'll want a baitcasting reel with a high gear ratio for fishing lures like crankbaits that cover lots of water and move quickly. Another consideration is whether you'll be targeting fish that move fast or, if fishing around cover, where you need to gather line quickly to keep slack out of the line or control big fish.

Low gear ratios are great for fishing spinnerbaits, worms or jerkbaits—lures that you work slowly and consistently, and for targeting gamefish in open water. When choosing a baitcasting reel, try to pick the reel that is the most applicable to the species you're targeting and the fishing technique you'll be using. In a pinch, you can use a high speed reel for fishing slow and a slow speed reel for cranking fast, but it requires more effort and awareness of the reel's performance.

For braided line (gel-spun polyethylene), many of the fishing reel manufacturers have beefed up drag systems to handle a heavier line-breaking strength than in the past. This allows anglers to fish smaller, lighter reels on their rods with similar line capacities using braided lines, yet a stronger drag system.

Spinning Reels

As with choosing a baitcasting reel, when selecting the right spinning reels for your fishing applications you want to consider line capacity, gear ratio and size (weight). Line capacity should be your single largest consideration, because it will often be the determining factor in whether or not you land a hooked fish. Because smaller reels can now withstand the stress of braided lines that have a smaller line diameter than monofilament but a stronger breaking strength, you can now use a smaller, lighter reel for many sight-fishing applications. Smaller and lighter mean more comfort over the course of a day, and that really makes a big difference when you spend the entire day holding your rod and reel or making lots of casts.

Reel size and weight are big considerations when sight casting to gamefish, whether that's looking along an offshore weedline for cobia or firing a shrimp and splitshot combination at small bonefish. At all times you want to keep your tackle sporting, yet having the right tools for the job will improve your chances of hooking and landing big fish.

In most cases, you can drop down a size in reel if you are using braided line because of its smaller diameter, which will give you more line capacity than with monofilament line. You may make hundreds of casts during a day on the water, and the lighter, smaller reel will contribute less to arm fatigue while remaining equally as effective.

In most cases, you'll want to choose a fishing reel that has the combination of the right line capacity for your target, a good gear ratio and the smallest size that's applicable for that line. In all cases, you want a reel with a super smooth drag, because a drag that bogs down or sticks will regularly break off powerful fish.

Long rods are used for casting distance with spinning reels. The rod must be loaded, as seen here, to spring forward and shoot the bait out.

When selecting spinning reels, consider line capacity, gear ratio, size and weight.

Spinning outfits, right, are popular for casting lightweight baits and lures for distance.

More powerful drags, lighter and smaller bodies, and improved spooling mechanisms have been primary advances in spinning reel design recently. What would have been considered a light seatrout or redfish spinning reel two decades ago, by its size, now has enough drag power and spool capacity to match up against nearshore species like kingfish and cobia.

These technical improvements make it easier for anglers to find reels that they can cast comfortably all day and use by touch. After all, one primary rule of sight fishing is that you don't want to take your eyes off the fish when you're preparing to make a cast. In that split instant you lose sight of the fish, you might well lose it for good.

Components of a reel's quality include how well—smoothly and evenly—it winds line onto its spool. That is crucial for the free flow of line off the reel during the cast, especially with the increased use of braided line with its tendency to loop onto itself and knot or tangle itself on a poorly-wound spool.

Likewise, the dependability of the bail—de-signed to catch the line for the retrieve—means nearly everything for the ensuing retrieve. Many practiced anglers not only clear the line from the spool by hand after the cast, but they set the bail manually. Taken together, these actions minimize the spinning reel's variable performance qualities, at least compared to a baitcaster. Bailess spinning reels are the logical next progression of this practice and increasingly in use. In everything from how it fits into your hand to how it lets you control line at all times, the reel's purpose is to provide good line maintenance at every turn.

Choosing the Right Fishing Line

The choice between monofilament and braided line isn't a difficult one. Each has its distinct advantages and disadvantages, and again, it's basically a personal choice. There are times when the advantages of a fishing line can skew the fishing in your favor. What you want to consider are the properties of each line, and then determine which style of line offers the best applications for the techniques you apply and fish you target most.

Nylon monofilament fishing line has been the standard of the fishing industry for over 50 years, and it offers some distinct advantages over other lines, the largest being that it stretches. Line stretch makes a big difference when fighting fish, particularly large fish that make powerful surges and long runs. If you make a mistake when fighting powerful fish like tarpon or marlin, the stretch of the monofilament line will often allow you the time to make the adjustments.

The drawback to line stretch is most often apparent when setting the hook. If you make a super long cast with monofilament and a fish strikes immediately, when you set the hook, the line will stretch from the stress. There are times when that stretch is just enough to keep the barb of the hook from penetrating the jaw of a fish.

Monofilament line is also thicker than braided line, which means you can't put as much line on your reel. But if you need more spool capacity, you can easily move up a reel size to get the extra line you need for fighting a big fish.

Many anglers who fish monofilament line on a regular basis just love the feel and sound of the line as it runs through the guides of the rod, along with the stretch. And because monofilament line has a larger diameter, it's often easier to untangle knots with it compared to braided line.

All that being said, braided line offers the angler some distinct advantages that can't be overlooked. The most prevalent among those advantages is the thinner diameter of the line per pound of breaking strength. Ten-pound braided line is usually the diameter of 2- to 4-pound monofilament line. That

Gel-spun polyethylene lines have become increasingly popular. Hybrid braided lines, below, containing new fiber blends, are constantly being developed and introduced to the market.

means a spinning reel that is designed to hold 130 yards of 10-pound monofilament line will hold double or more of the braided line.

Equally important is that the thinner braided line casts like thinner monofilament. That means you can make longer casts with braided line and fish lighter lures or baits. That's a huge advantage over monofilament.

Any time you're sight fishing you are casting to a fish that has the potential to see you and react negatively to your presence, so you always want to make the longest cast possible. Longer casts also allow you to cover more water with your retrieve, allowing more time for the fish to decide whether it wants to eat a lure or bait. So as a general

Braided lines have their pros and cons for inshore anglers, but they're showing up on more spools.

rule, longer casts are a distinct advantage with many forms of sight fishing.

The thinner diameter of braided line makes it more difficult for fish to see, particularly in the smaller line tests, but that also means it's more difficult for the angler to see, which makes it tough to untangle knots or track a hooked fish's movements in the water. Monofilament and braided lines are available in high visibility colors that improve the ability of an angler to track the line, but even with these bright neon colors, a light braided line can be difficult to see in the water.

Unlike monofilament, braided line does not stretch, which offers advantages and disadvantages. A big advantage comes when a fish strikes at the beginning of a retrieve following a long cast. When there is a lot of line between the angler and the fish, the elasticity of mono may impede hooksets. Braided line better transmits immediate hook-setting force. On the other hand, because the line doesn't stretch, it's easier to pop a fish off by setting the hook too hard, or having the drag too tight with a surging fish. You'll want to choose between the stretch and visibility of monofilament and the line capacity, improved casting distance and hooksetting power of braided line.

One last line composition to consider is fluorocarbon (extruded polyvinylidene fluoride). Fluorocarbon has less reflective properties and is a little denser than nylon monofilament, which means it's harder for the fish to see and sinks a little faster. There are applications when sight fishing in super clear water where fluorocarbon offers a major advantage, the most common of which is sight casting to bass in very clear, shallow water. When the water gets super clear, 10-pound nylon monofilament and even the thin diameter braided lines will stand out, particularly if you are fishing a lure or bait that will sit directly in a fish's field of vision for prolonged periods of time. That is when fluorocarbon line comes into its own, but it is a limited application.

Another application for fluorocarbon line is when fishing worms or crankbaits, lures that you want to sink or swim at a specific depth. Because the line sinks, you get a truer level of retrieve when working those baits, and usually have to allow less time before starting the retrieve.

Fluorocarbon leader stands up fairly well to the raspy mouth of a snook and other abrasions.

Leader Materials

As long as we're talking about fluorocarbon lines, we should discuss the single most consistent application for the property of the line, which is low visibility. There's no denying that fluorocarbon lines are more difficult for fish to see underwater, so it has definite advantages when used in conjunction with monofilament or braided lines.

In super clear (or even in tannic stained) water, fish are less likely to detect fluorocarbon than monofilament or braided line, so you can utilize fluorocarbon to improve upon the properties of the other lines. Adding a fluorocarbon leader to monofilament or braided line often results in more bites from fish because it distances the thicker monofilament and opaque braided line from the vision of the fish.

How long that leader material needs to be depends on the fish and the visibility of the water. Let's say you're fishing blue ocean water and sight casting to a cobia swimming slowly across the top of a wreck. You are using live bait and 30-pound-test bright yellow, high visibility braided or monofilament line. With a normal monofilament leader or steel leader, that fish may swim up to investigate the baitfish which remains in its field of vision for several seconds. During that time, the fish will see the bright line in the water along with the monofilament or steel leader tethering it. You'll know that the cobia knows something's wrong because it will nose or push the bait without eating it. You can adjust to the situation by dropping down in breaking strength of your leader and increasing its length, but once the fish has its guard up it's more difficult to get it to eat.

Adding a long fluorocarbon leader to the line decreases the visibility of the leader and the connection to the high visibility line. Any time you're using high visibility line you want to increase the length of your leader, so in this case, a 4- to 6-foot length of fluorocarbon leader will put the high visibility line out of the fish's range of vision while producing an almost invisible connection.

Using fluorocarbon for leader material also has some good applications when you want a lure or bait to sink. Because fluorocarbon line is heavier than nylon monofilament or braided line, it sinks faster. So when you are sight casting a rubber worm to a bass in super clear water where you can't use a weight because the fish will see it, you can add a piece of fluorocarbon leader. Fluorocarbon will make it more difficult for the bass to detect the line and also allow the worm to sink below the surface. You'll see this application in a lot of clear lakes

> **Another application for fluorocarbon is fishing worms or crankbaits, lures that you want at specific depths.**

Think about the composition of your leader material and what performance qualities you want from it.

when fishing bass in shallow water.

So fluorocarbon line has distinct advantages when used as leader material, particularly in super clear water. The main disadvantage is that fluorocarbon is more expensive than monofilament line, and anglers may feel the extra cost doesn't outweigh the advantages.

Fluorocarbon lines tend to be very stiff, while monofilament has a variety of properties. Some monofilaments are super stiff, while others are supple. There are applications for each.

Stiff nylon monofilament is often used when fishing large saltwater gamefish like tarpon that have small abrasive teeth, much like sandpaper, that will saw through a softer line during a prolonged battle. The drawback to the stiffer monofilament is that it is usually easier for the fish

to see and has a lot of memory, so it must be pre-straightened before use. You can also drop down a category of line strength to compensate for the higher visibility of the stiff monofilament, but in most cases, the abrasion resistance is what anglers are seeking from this leader material.

Soft, supple monofilament leader material is great for fish that don't have teeth because it avoids kinks and is harder for the fish to detect. You'll see this type of monofilament utilized when targeting fish like striped bass, seatrout and calico bass, where the fish are less likely to sever the leader over the course of a long fight.

What of tinted monofilament or fluorocarbon? Some line companies offer their leader materials in different colors. Various shades of red are favored by some bluewater anglers, while grays or brown are popular with the nearshore and inshore crowds. Red is the first color to disappear from the light spectrum when underwater, so many bluewater anglers feel red or clear blue offer the lowest visibility in the clear blue waters of the ocean. Inshore waters are often stained green or brown, which is why the gray or brown leader materials excel in these conditions. Then again, clear leader does well in most fishing applications.

Any time you're going sight fishing you should think about the composition of your leader material and whether you're looking for low visibility, abrasion resistance, sinking properties or color. All these factors, along with leader length should be considered before you ever make your first cast at a fish. After all, when you spend the effort to locate fish and position yourself to make a good cast to it, you don't want to have that lure or bait denied.

Fluorocarbon lines—less visible, greater abrasion resistance.

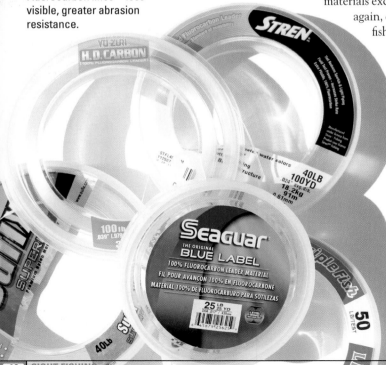

In clear water, presentations call for leaders as invisible as possible to fool a permit.

Fly Tackle Considerations

The art of sight fishing with hook and line is rooted deepest in fly fishing. You see, the spin- and baitcasting tackle familiar to so many coastal and freshwater anglers is relatively new to the fishing scene.

As far back as the early 15th century, fishermen in the British Isles were using hand-crafted poles with horsehair line to take dace, tench, trout and other small species. Much of the fishing was what we'd today call "blind-fishing," soaking a bait on bottom in a likely area, or beneath a float. But among the "six ways of angling" espoused by early fishing writer Dame Juliana Berners in *A Treatise on Fishing with an Angle* (1420), we come to the sixth: "And if you see at any time of day the trout or grayling leap, angle for him with an artificial fly appropriate for that month."

It's doubtful Berners' readers regarded themselves as "fly fishermen" per se—and their gear would bear little resemblance to today's fly tackle—but nevertheless the image stuck. Particularly the "seeing" aspect of Berners' sixth way.

The term "fly" is a little misleading: The insect hatch-match embodied in early fly fishing history has broadened to include a wide range of imitative patterns. Today we have flies tied to represent minnows, crabs, shrimp. . . even popular lures (spoon flies! MirrOlure flies!). One common thread, if you will, is nominal weight, so that the delivery of the "fly" from caster to target may be imparted only by the momentum of the fly line.

Some fish, like bonefish, tarpon and bass are fly friendly, meaning that they will readily take a well-presented fly, whereas other species like billfish, tuna and king mackerel require live chumming or

The art of sight fishing with hook and line is rooted deepest in fly fishing.

a bait-and-switch technique. One advantage of flies is that they sink slowly or are neutral-balanced so that they can be paused and remain in the strike zone for prolonged periods of time. Some days, it seems, if you keep food in front of a fish's face long enough, it will eventually decide to eat.

When it comes to choosing the best fly rod for your fishing applications there are a few things to consider: size of the fish you plan to target, size of the flies you're casting, and the distance you will cast. Each of these variables will determine the size, weight and length of the fly rod you will use, although many fly rods have multiple applications.

For instance, most anglers targeting large tarpon on the flats or beaches utilize a 12-weight rod, while anglers targeting redfish on the flats use an 8-weight rod and anglers after brown trout in a large stream throw a 6-weight. But these applications

change along with the variables of the size of the fish and locations you're fishing. Smaller tarpon, say 30 to 50 pounds, may demand flies best delivered with a 9-weight rod. At the same time, a redfish angler may desire a 9-weight rod for applying more pressure to breeding-size redfish that

can reach 40 pounds. If those brown trout were in a small stream, sipping tiny midges in still pools, then a 4- or 5-weight rod might be more suitable. In essence, you want to match the size of the rod to the size of the fish you're targeting, but that's not the complete story.

The size or weight of the fly you plan to use is relative to rod selection in that a heavier or larger (bulkier) fly is usually easier to cast with a heavier fly line and rod. Weighted flies like those used for permit don't cast well on an 8-weight rod, and even though you might be targeting 10- to 15-pound fish in open water, a 9- or 10-weight rod is a better option because it will produce more efficient casts with the heavy fly.

Larger, bulkier flies designed to represent baitfish like mullet, or large poppers designed to create a lot of surface commotion, both create a lot of drag in the air so they often cast better with a rod one size heavier than the normal option. What that means is, if you're targeting snook in a situation that would normally require an 8-weight rod but are using a big baitfish pattern, you're likely going to get more strikes using a 9-weight rod because it will cast the fly easier and farther. The farther you can cast the less likely a fish will detect your

presence and spook from the fly.

As for fly reels, there are good reels on the market today, and even the inexpensive models have the features that provide great sport when sight fishing. As with spinning and baitcasting tackle, you want to make sure any reel you use has a good, smooth drag, as any sticking or hanging up while a fish surges will surely break that fish off.

The choice of large or small arbor for the reel is relative to the length of the run the fish will make and how aggressive you want to be while fighting it. For large fish like billfish, tuna and even tarpon, a large arbor reel is a great asset that will help you land a fish in a timely manner, thus increasing the chance of survival when released. Large arbor reels allow you to gain considerably more line with every crank of the reel handle than a small arbor reel, but in many applications a large arbor reel is overkill.

The major differences between expensive and relatively affordable fly reels are in the strength and durability of the materials and the quality of the drag system. Since the drag is one of the most important factors with any fishing reel, you'll want to purchase the best reel you can afford so that you know it will last the test of time and be just as effective at fighting and catching fish years down the road.

Fly lines are another consideration when purchasing a fly fishing outfit. In most cases you want to match the size of the line to the size of the rod, but not always. Overlining a rod with a fly line one size larger may help you get extra distance from your casting, but results will differ among casters and rod makes. The slightly heavier fly line works particularly well in a stiff wind.

For the most part, floating fly lines are used when sight fishing. But, the slow-sinking "intermediate" lines have some special applications, such as tracking straight beneath surface chop while tarpon fishing, or taking a streamer fly down to the level of snook visible along a bridge.

When all the angler's efforts in tackle, technique and timing come together at the scene of the hookup, the work of sport is rewarded. Left, Spanish macks will chase synthetic streamer flies, at left, lower.

CHAPTER 4

Locating Fish

Fish are creatures of habit, and as you spend more time looking for them, you'll find that areas or scenarios that produce fish in one region will also hold fish in another. As you stock your mental inventory of these little nuances, your senses become naturally heightened as you search out the fish that should be in the area. Reading the water, knowing the influence of tides and water temperatures, and the importance of structure and shorelines all pay off for the sight fisherman.

Understanding the habits of fish and the factors that control their movements will allow you to effectively spot and present baits to fish.

On a calm day off-shore, top, finding a sargassum weedline should pay off. Right, gamefish are often seen by docklights.

The Strike Points

In stream trout fishing, big fish like to hold in the downstream eddy of a boulder or rock that cuts the water current and flows food around one side of the structure. A trout can sit behind that rock and expend little energy, remaining out of the stream current, while waiting for its food to come naturally across its field of vision. After seeing that scenario several times, you'll naturally gravitate toward rocks or boulders in the middle of a stream, looking into the downcurrent eddy for fish.

What you'll find over time is that understanding the habits of fish and the factors that control their movements will allow you to more effectively spot and present baits to fish. Below are some of the little nuances common to sight fishing.

Changes in the Water

Depending on the species you're targeting, the water color, depth and clarity will often determine where the fish hold. This may be something as apparent as an offshore color change where the

Stream angler in New Zealand fishes the run by the head of a pool, where trout likely lie looking for food delivered by water flow.

water changes dramatically from green to blue or as simple as a layer of dirty water on the surface where the fish lie deeper in the clearer water where they can see their prey much better. These factors are species dependent.

For instance, snook and largemouth bass like to hold in tannin-stained water along the edge of clear water where they can lurk relatively undetected and lunge out at prey swimming along the clear side of the edge. Species like spotted seatrout would prefer to sit in the crystal clear water where they can see any approaching predators as well as their prey from long distances.

One of the most striking examples of distinct color changes in the water is an offshore color change, which may be representative of a temperature break, current flow or clash of waters of different quality (salinity, nutrient levels, origins). Bluewater gamefish regularly prefer one side of the color change over the other, and will hunt the preferred side, and knowing this can dramatically decrease the amount of water you have to cover to find fish.

These fish will regularly hunt down one side of the color change looking for food moving from one level of water clarity to the other. Sight casting to fish in blue water is extremely difficult because of the volume of water the fish can hold in and because only so much water holds fish. Color changes do give definitive location to where fish will hunt (along the color change), so they help define the areas where you're most likely to encounter the fish you're after.

Also, the clearer the water, the easier it

Anglers in Cuba wade to a trench in a flat where fish gather. Below, distinct offshore color change with weeds.

is to identify a fish and position yourself to make a good cast. Fish regularly seek out the cleaner water because it improves their field of vision and allows them to see any predators as they get close. These factors allow fish to relax and feed comfortably, which is an important factor when trying to get a fish to eat.

Hunt Shorelines

Shorelines are natural fish attractors for several reasons: they hold a variety of prey; limit the avenues of escape for that prey; and usually present great ambush points. As fish grow, they learn that shorelines are locations to catch their food, so they spend more time hunting near them.

Shorelines also make great locations for sight casting fish. The relatively shallow water and limited area along shorelines allow anglers to pinpoint where fish will hold and position themselves to be able to see the fish and cast to it before the fish detects their presence. That may mean approaching from deeper water or from land, but in either instance you approach at an angle from the fish's peripheral vision so the fish is less likely to see any movement or sense your presence and move off.

Along shorelines there are usually two types of fish feeding scenarios: stationary fish that are waiting to lunge at their prey and moving fish that are looking to hunt down their prey. Both scenarios are effective for sight casting.

Stationary fish are common with "grasping" predators like spotted seatrout, bass, snook, redfish and quite frequently, freshwater trout. All of these species will also feed by moving along a shoreline. The key to seeing stationary fish before they detect your presence is to move slowly and deliberately at all times while watching ahead for fish. This type of fishing may manifest itself in saltwater when anglers are poling a boat along a shoreline or wading and casting toward mangroves. Gamefish will position themselves along the shorelines, usually in areas with moving water so that their prey is washed into striking distance with the tide or current. These fish typically face into the current, and are completely focused on what is coming down the current directly in front of their faces, so they're much easier to approach from downcurrent or to the deeper side of the fish. From there,

the key is to put the lure, bait or fly upcurrent of the fish so that it will flow naturally within striking range without having the fish see your movements.

Fish moving along a shoreline are much harder to target because the window of opportunity is smaller as the fish moves closer to you. Fish movement constantly changes the angle and distance of the cast. You can target these fish by remaining stationary and waiting for them to come by, which gives you a consistent casting angle, or you can

Narrow canals, rich with life, offer few ambush points for fish. They'll hug the banks. Right, inshore anglers check downed trees along a channeled-out flat.

move in the opposite direction that the fish are hunting, thus approaching them and closing the ground you have to cover. In either instance, you want to remain stationary any time you spot fish, and then cast ahead of the moving fish.

A common scenario is sight casting to redfish or snook moving down a shoreline or to jack crevalle chasing mullet against a seawall. In all these instances the fish are looking to approach their prey from the outside, forcing it toward the shoreline and eliminating avenues of escape. A cast to the shoreline side of the fish is the one that will draw a strike.

Gamefish position themselves along the shorelines, usually in areas with moving water so that their prey washes to them.

Temperature Factors

Air temperatures and sun levels control water temperatures, which thus affect the habits of gamefish. For instance, when the air is hot, such as in summer, tropical fish like seatrout and snook feed more often early in the day when the sun is low and the water is at its coolest period after cooling down overnight. Conversely, in the winter months, a snook will feed more in the afternoons when the air has warmed the water and the fish are more active.

Water temperature affects individual species differently, and it's up to you to learn the habits of the gamefish you're targeting, which will significantly increase your odds of success. After all, looking for feeding fish at a time of day when they aren't going to be feeding is not a great way to sight cast to gamefish.

Just about every gamefish has a temperature range when it is most active, and you want to be fishing when that temperature is at its optimum level. For muskellunge, that is when the

Pike go on the feed in cool weather, left, often looking for food among the shallow grasses in northern waters.

water is cool during the summer months and warm during the winter months, much like snook. For tarpon, it's a specific temperature (80 degrees) that you're looking for, no matter the season. That's their zone of comfort. If there's a cold water upwelling along the beach and the water is 65 degrees, you're better served to move on (often miles) until you find a water temperature closer to the 80-degree mark.

Fishing a backcountry mangrove zone in cool weather. Fish will be near the culvert outflow coursing with food.

For sight fishing along the beaches, that same cold water upwelling that moves the tarpon schools away from the area will force to the surface cobia that have been shadowing stingrays on the bottom. The fish rise to avoid the extreme cold. When schools of cobia come to the surface to warm up (usually in the middle of the day), they're considerably easier to spot and sight cast than when they are holding to a ray on the bottom. In this scenario the cold water plays to the favor of the sight casting angler.

Extreme instances of cold water can shut down a gamefish's body functions, making it lethargic and unwilling to feed, and can thus shut down the bite even while making them easier to locate. In extreme cases, fish will be killed by sudden and extreme dips in water temperatures. If the fish you're after are made lethargic by cold, you're better off moving on and chasing a species that is more cold temperature tolerant or finding the pockets of warm water that are holding fish still wanting to eat. Inversely, coldwater species such as rainbow trout are apt to gather near springs or shady riffles as a refuge from midsummer warming of streams.

Temperature also plays a factor in the visibility of the water, particularly in salt water, which contains a lot of diatoms. Prolonged periods of cold weather during the winter months will kill the diatoms in the water, which then sink and settle to the bottom, decreasing the amount of matter in the water layer and making the water much clearer. That's one of the main reasons anglers encounter such great sightfishing conditions inshore during the winter months.

Also remember that cold water is denser than warm water which makes it heavier, which is why you regularly find thermoclines deep into the water column. Knowing that the warmer water is going to be on top, you can expect to find fish that prefer warmer conditions on the surface and colder conditions down deep.

Water temperature affects individual species differently, and it's up to you to learn the habits of the gamefish you're after.

Structure Holds Fish

Many gamefish are structure-oriented, which is to say they gravitate to specific structure like weed beds, rocks, grass, docks or pilings or mangroves. That structure may be fixed, as with trees or weed beds, or moving as in weedlines flowing in current offshore. In either instance, the gamefish move to the structure for safety and food.

Shoreline structure can be some of the most consistent areas for sight casting gamefish because it's easily accessible from land or boat. Good examples of shoreline structure are rock jetties, rockpiles, piers and docks. Small fish and baitfish gravitate toward structure for the safety it provides from predators, and gamefish move to these structures for those food items.

Just about every dock or fishing pier has small fish that hold around it, and these structures provide shade during the middle of the day. Keep in mind that fish don't have eyelids, so when the sun

Gamefish move to the structure for safety and food.

A kayaker has anchored at a good approach position near timber along a shore and attempts to tease a fish out of hiding there.

Jetties are always magnets for bait fish and gamefish. Reading currents around rocks is key.

is high in the sky the light is hard on their eyes and they have to move to deeper water or shade any time they want to decrease the amount of light in their eyes. In the shallows hunting food, they'll use the high light for locating and tracking prey.

Around structure, you want to be observant of any current. Fish like to face into the current when they feed, so current direction and strength will be determining factors when trying to locate gamefish. Some fish species will sit on the upcurrent side of the structure, while others regularly prefer the downcurrent side. Knowing the habits of the fish gives the angler a good idea where they will be stationed.

When fishing structure like rockpiles and jetties there will be locations where the fish like to hold during specific tides, often because the current pushes baitfish or other food items into that spot. Many times that's an eddy out of the current or off a point in the land—a place where the current wraps around the rocks and pushes food items with it. Fish congregate at the ambush points and may strike out at the food. When you have that scenario, you'll usually find fish in that location on a regular basis.

In moving water scenarios, the best approach is rarely head-on. Keep in mind that the fish is facing forward, so that a head-on approach moves the angler into the main field of vision for the fish. If that fish is feeding on something that is flowing in the current, it's difficult to drift or work a lure or bait downcurrent to the fish with it looking natural. So approach from one side or the other, often from downcurrent and at a right angle so when the cast lands you are working the lure or bait back toward the fish utilizing the current.

There are also scenarios where current doesn't play a factor around structure, as with weed beds or around mangroves. Fish sitting stationary in these locations, like a bass holding in a pothole of weeds or a snook stationary under some mangroves, are still very catchable. You want to pick an angle where the cast will work the bait into

> ## When fishing structure like rockpiles and jetties there will be distinct locations where the fish like to hold during specific tides, often because of current action.

The pools at the base of a fall are trout feeding stations. Here, a stream in Pennsylvania.

the fish's line of vision, again without positioning yourself in the main field of vision, so that the fish thinks the offering moved into its strike zone.

Offshore anglers often fish around structure as well, targeting artificial reefs, oil rigs, channel markers and floating buoys. Fish like barracuda, cobia and permit sit on the surface around artificial reefs and wrecks, while tripletail will hold on the downcurrent side of channel markers and buoys. In these scenarios, as with most sight casting situations, the key element in your success will be the approach. If you can spot your target from a distance, approach it slowly and at an angle that will keep you and your movements out of the main field of vision, and then make a cast into their strike

zone, you will have success on a regular basis. Try to make it a general rule to stop the boat a good distance from the structure and approach it slowly, allowing the anglers to spot the fish before the fish detects their presence, and then position the boat for the best presentation to the fish.

Freshwater sight fishing scenarios are no different. When sight fishing along weedlines you want to look for fish sitting on the edges of the weeds if there's a distinct edge, which you'll find in many of the freshwater lakes around the country. Bass and other gamefish will move in and out of the grass, using the grass as a hiding spot to ambush baitfish as they move by. When you see bass move under the grass, you can cast to the edge of the grass and draw a strike from those fish.

Feeding Stations

Feeding stations are locations to which fish regularly move when looking for food. That may be a dropoff along a flat, a particular rock in a stream or a current edge offshore adjacent to a reef line. All these areas draw gamefish because they regularly hold food, and give the fish some strategic advantage, minimizing the expense of energy required to catch prey.

Because these feeding stations yield food sources on a consistent basis you'll find that not just one or two fish, but many fish of all sizes will utilize that location to feed. If you see and catch a fish from that location one day, in the future that fish will likely be replaced by another because of the consistent food source. Fish gravitate toward consistent food, whether that's a piling around a bridge where the current delivers crabs, or a big sand hole in a massive grass flat where the tide dumps shrimp into the deeper water on the outgoing tide. Learn these feeding stations and fish them frequently, and you'll have great success.

A good scenario for targeting tarpon or permit in the Florida Keys is to find them gulping crabs off the surface in the current between two islands or along the deep edge of a dropoff between two shallow grassflats. Because the water is deeper it will move more current and water volume which will stack up the weeds and tide in those areas. As the weeds flow through on the tide they are carrying shrimp and crabs which utilize those weeds as protection and their main means of locomotion. Tarpon and permit will hold on the surface or just below it facing into the current as they watch for food to come by on the weeds.

Anglers can see these fish feeding in one location on a regular basis on certain tide phases. Day after day, the fish will follow the same patterns, and anglers can position their boat to one side of the fish and make a cast upcurrent to allow their offering to flow directly into the fish's feeding window. When that offering comes floating through, the fish think it's just another piece of the natural food chain, and are quick to strike. It's not at all unlike freshwater trout choosing "lanes" in a stream that optimize their view of various insect life stages passing by on the current. SB

Gamefish approach feeding stations from specific directions. Knowing how the fish you're targeting feed in any given location allows you to approach it from an angle where the fish is less likely to detect your presence while providing the best casting angle to get the bait in front of the fish and moving along the natural avenues of approach.

A redfish's dorsal and tail are clearly visible above the surface. Now it's up to the angler, right, to place the cast properly.

CHAPTER 5

Spotting Fish

Most gamefish have excellent eyesight, and in super clear water will see an angler making erratic movements from a good distance. Even normal casting actions, shadows of the anglers, boat noises or the approach of a boat can easily set some fish on their guard. Therefore one of the most important efforts when sight casting is to minimize your physical profile.

The thing to remember here is that fish have predators too, many of which come from above the water, such as birds, sea lions, bears and of course, man. From the earliest stages of their lives they learn to watch for the approach of predators above and below the water and to seek sanctuary when danger approaches, so fish often get edgy at the first hint of something unusual.

By taking your time, moving slowly and making calculated movements, you will get closer to fish than you ever imagined.

Angler at the
ready on a casting
platform, scanning a
seagrass flat.

How Your Movement Will Spook and Expose Fish

As an angler, it is imperative that you always make slow, deliberate movements any time you are searching out fish. Often, it's best to move slow and calculate your approach to any area that can potentially hold fish. The more experienced you get at sight fishing, the more you'll realize that fish will bust away scared from just about any erratic movement. Even when you take your time they will detect your presence.

Fish aren't as easy to spot as you'd think. Most game-fish have the colorations that reflect their natural environments so they blend into the background. It's not so easy to spot a green bass along a weed bed, a copper redfish over a mud bottom or a sailfish in ocean water.

What you will find is that by taking your time, moving slowly and making calculated move-ments, you will get closer to fish than you ever imagined possible. Fish that you didn't see until your boat or feet were directly on them won't see you either. That is, until you just about run them over. You'll also find that fish movements are the single best way to spot fish.

Fish sitting stationary will blend into their environment given their natural colorations. A redfish waiting under mangroves or a seatrout sitting over mud or sand bottom is almost impossible to detect until you get close. Same for permit over sand, brown trout over pebbles and bass around weeds. You rarely catch fish if you spook them before you can cast to them. Keep that in mind at all times, and you'll learn to slow down and really scan an area for fish before you move.

Even when you take your time and approach fish silently, the act of casting will at times spook

In still water where the redfish sits by man-groves, top, and on flats with slow flow, right, even slight movements by anglers can put fish in a wary mode.

Poling to fish on the feed, like these redfish from a school, allows for a near silent and stealthy approach.

Seatrout—one of the top gamefish nearshore in the Southeast and Gulf states—can be effectively sight fished.

Seatrout sitting motionless along the shoreline look exactly like a big mangrove log in the mud, and five or six look like a regular log jam!

fish. Spotted seatrout and bonefish are notorious for spotting the movement of a casting angler and moving off. As you learn the habits of the species and what they react to, you'll also learn how much you can move when making the cast.

Just about any time you're in close proximity to a gamefish you'll want to make the quickest casting movement possible, which can be a real test when throwing a fly that requires several cycles of the rod to load the line. One of the best ways to combat fish seeing your casting action is to change the casting angle so that you are in the fish's peripheral vision and not directly in front of it. A fish that is focused on food being swept downcurrent directly in front of its face will likely never see your approach from the side, but will react to any movement from a good distance when head-on. If you find that fish are regularly detecting your approach or casting movements, then change your angle of approach, and look for fish while moving in that angle.

Any time you are looking for fish, move slowly and look for fish that are moving. As fish move into an area to hunt, they regularly

cover water and throw wakes as they work the shoreline or other type of structure looking for prey. Keep a keen eye for that movement, as it exposes fish from great distances.

Schooling fish are the greatest opportunity for this scenario. Redfish, for example, will move along at times as a big school, with the fish changing direction and actively pursuing prey as they cross the flat. I remember taking a good friend to a spot along a dark, muddy shoreline that held about two dozen redfish. The fish we saw were close to shore holding stationary in a small depression just inside of a shallow sandbar. Because the water was so shallow (less than a foot), my buddy never thought of looking there, and even when I pointed to the fish, he couldn't see them because they were sitting motionless over the dark bottom. But when one fish moved forward to eat a shrimp, the other fish reacted to that movement, just a few inches, but enough that my friend could now see them. He caught his first redfish on his first cast, and watched the fish swim up and eat his lure. To this day he says it's one of the most memorable catches of his life.

Popping cork sprays water near a sandy depression in a seagrass bed—likely haunt for lurking seatrout, above.

See Shapes to Spot Fish

The more time you spend stalking and sight casting to fish, the better you get at spotting those fish at a distance. What you realize over time is that your eyes become accustomed to looking in specific areas for fish—places that are naturally fishy and hold fish—and also for specific shapes. Spotted seatrout are a good example.

In the winter months, I look for large seatrout in super shallow water over mud bottom. Those fish come into the shallows to get warm, and are specifically looking for the darker colored mud which the sun will naturally heat up quicker than lighter sand or grass bottom. These fish sit motionless along the shorelines and near the mangroves warming up as they watch for an easy meal to come within striking distance.

Because the fish don't move much, they're harder to detect than the redfish and snook in the area that are constantly moving forward and looking for a meal. Without that movement to expose their presence, I have to rely on the one thing that sets them apart from the brown mud (mud is the same color as the fish's backs), and that's their shape.

Gator seatrout sitting motionless along the shoreline look exactly like a big mangrove log

Tell Tale Signs You Can't Miss

It's the dream scenario for the sight fishing angler—the tails are above the surface and the fish are feeding. But what species is it? Get to know the distinctive shapes and movements of top gamefish so that you're ready when they appear. Here are shots of three species as they tail—bonefish, permit and redfish.

The bonefish, moving to the right, has sharp, triangular fins, colored silver, gray or greenish gray. When feeding vigorously, its tail quivers quickly, and at times in deeper water its dorsal may be submerged and only its tail fin exposed.

Permit can be fast foragers, even on the flats, though they will nose down to root out food for some duration. Their dorsal and tail fins are sickle-shaped, silvery and yellowish, and the dorsals of big permit may flop over when exposed to the air.

Redfish dorsal fin is broad and thick, tinged reddish or orange, almost resembling a sail. Redfish jut side to side in a narrow path as they feed on the move, giving the tail a jerking movement.

in the mud, and five or six of those trout look like a regular log jam! But you don't see a lot of mangrove logs in the water in my area, so more often than not, what appears to be logs in the water along the shore are big seatrout sitting stationary over the mud. Knowing this, I approach anything that looks like a log as if it's a fish, and determine the best angle to make the longest cast possible. In that way, I catch a lot of big trout, and a handful of big logs.

The deep V of a permit's tail is visible beneath greenish tinted water, and its two-tone body color, darker above, also shows well.

The more time you spend sight fishing the better you get at it and at determining the specific outline shapes of the fish you pursue. Muskies sitting on the edge of a grass bed look like suspended shadows, cobia on the back of a turtle look like brown sharks and tarpon laid-up in shallow cover appear as green pilings. Each fish has a distinct shape and coloration that will help you see it.

Permit are another good example of shapes that I see long before I get a good look at the fish. Permit have reflective sides, but very pronounced white lips and a dark V-shaped tail. Depending on which way they face, they give a specific shape profile. Permit approaching head-on will look like sets of white lips in the water while permit moving away will look like dark Vs swimming away. More often than not, I will see the white lips or dark V tail long before I see the rest of the fish, and making a cast to those shapes will yield a bite because the fish haven't gotten close enough to you to detect your presence.

Colors Are Key

Look for specific colors. This can be particularly effective when fish are traveling in large schools. This is a technique you'll use on a regular basis when sight fishing specific gamefish or locations whether that be on the beach, offshore, inshore or even in fresh water.

A solitary fish swimming several feet deep may be difficult to spot even when the colorations on the back of the fish are different than the color of the water and its surroundings, but put an entire school of those fish together and they really stand out. If that school is on the surface, they can be seen for hundreds of yards.

Every spring in Southeast Florida we see schools of large jack crevalle gathering along the beaches to spawn. These schools may hold over 1,000 fish averaging 20 to 30 pounds, and when that school is on the surface the yellow sides and light brown backs of the fish create a large dark spot in the green water. That spot is brighter when the fish are on the surface, and darker when the fish move deep. Knowing that, anglers can run the beaches watching for dark spots in the water and then approach those areas quietly to sight cast fish.

The same goes for big schools of permit on the offshore wrecks. One fish swimming down deep might be difficult to see, but 40 of them will create a greenish hue in the water. That change in coloration allows anglers to know the location of the fish, and approach it slowly while being ready to cast to any fish that move higher into the water column. At times, a boat with a trolling motor can silently follow that permit school and wait for single fish to come to the surface to feed, and sight fish those individual fish.

Similar situations exist for schools of snook which look brown over sand, for bass and tarpon which look green over sand and cobia which look dark brown or black in contrast with the blue or green ocean water. In all these instances, the colorations of the fish make large differentiations in the color of the water to expose their presence.

But fish don't always have to be in a school for color to make them easy to spot. Mutton snapper cruising over a grassflat will have a very light brown or pinkish color, while spotted seatrout appear dark brown when over sand and redfish look almost black except for the pink in their

Fish don't have to be in a school for color to make them easy to spot.

Big jack crevalle, whose sporty fight is underappreciated by many anglers, gather in big schools by beaches along the Southeast and Gulf states.

A bonefish's stripes and shadow stand out against Bahamas bay bottom, but in a seagrass bed, good luck.

lighter as they move over the dark grass. In both these instances what you're looking for is a different shade of light or dark than what you're seeing with the surroundings, and then keying in on the spot where you're seeing that color to determine if it has an outline like a fish or a school of fish. As you get closer and focus on that color, the shape of the fish will come into view.

fins, the same pinkish fins that expose brook trout in a mountain stream.

At times, the variations in color are more along the lines of black and white, with the fish being darker or lighter than the natural surroundings. Snook along shorelines tend to be darker than their natural surroundings, and bonefish can be

You will learn the different colorations they exhibit that make them stand out against the background of their natural environments, and then you'll be able to key in on those differences in color to help you spot those fish. In time, it will get easier to spot fish by simply watching for specific shapes and colors as well as movement.

Fleeing baits give away the sailfish at right, but a sail on its own in blue water may go unseen by unpracticed eyes.

Above water, a snook's golden triangles of fins are easily spotted, but below the surface, the fish blends in well.

Watch for Other Species

Some gamefish like to hitchhike or piggyback with other fish as part of their natural movements. These fish utilize the marine creature they follow as a source of concealment as well as exposure to food. Probably the most common marine species that takes on hitchhikers are the southern stingray and the pelagic manta ray.

Rays swim at varied levels of the water column, with manta rays moving from surface to bottom, while the common stingrays hold tight to the bottom at all times. As these rays swim along the bottom, the natural action of flapping their wings for locomotion disturbs the bottom and exposes shrimp, crabs and other food items hiding in the sand. When the food items become exposed, the

Top, stingray has a fish following it to catch food bits the stingray kicks up. Bottom, a cast is made to a cobia below a manta ray off a southeast Florida beach.

fish swimming with the ray simply pins the snack to the bottom and consumes its meal.

Any time you're fishing saltwater grassflats you want to watch for stingrays moving across the grass in shallow water. Once you key in on the movement and direction of the stingray, you can watch it closely for any fish that are swimming with it. Quite often those fish will be right on the back of the ray making them difficult to spot, but they will also swim just behind the ray, particularly when looking for food items kicked up behind the ray by the movements of its wings.

If you see a redfish or other gamefish on the back of the ray, the best cast is either right in front of the ray or directly on the nose of the fish. Fish feeding on the backs of rays are looking for shrimp or crabs exposed by the motion of the ray's wings, and those tidbits pop up in front of the gamefish quickly, so a close cast will usually not spook the fish. Conversely, the feeding fish are so focused on watching for food to come sweeping up directly behind the ray that they may not see a bait cast to the side of the ray.

Stingrays in inshore waters are known to have mutton snapper, jack crevalle and redfish on their backs on a regular basis, but I've seen everything from pompano to bonefish traveling with these rays. (As an aside, unaccompanied stingrays are nevertheless a good sign of life on a flat.) Offshore stingrays are known for holding cobia, which depend on the rays to expose shrimp and crabs. Those cobia may be on the bottom with the ray, or they may come to the surface.

Manta rays also hold cobia, and when the rays come to the surface, the cobia will sometimes duck under the wings of the huge rays. The cobia may be difficult to see, which is why you always make a cast to big manta rays swimming on the surface—just in case there is a cobia. You might not see the cobia underneath, but a lure or bait cast just ahead and to the near-side of a manta ray may result in one or more cobia coming out and grabbing your offering.

Turtles are another marine animal that regularly have fish associated with them. Cobia will follow big leatherback turtles. Dolphin (mahi) will sometimes swim with the same species as well as with loggerhead and green turtles. In both instances, the fish will only be visible when the turtles are on the surface, so you want to approach turtles from behind or they will see you and dive down, taking the fish you're hoping to catch with them.

> **Keep an eye peeled for other species that may attract and shield gamefish from view.**

One way to increase your chances of catching a fish off the back of a turtle or ray is to cast a hookless teaser plug to the area and work it back to the boat while another angler gets ready to cast to any fish that follow the teaser. (It is also a great way to avoid hooking one of those half-ton creatures!) The standard hookless teaser can be any lure with some weight to it (usually 1 to 2 ounces), from a large pencil popper to an 8- or 9-inch soft-plastic eel. Because you can cast the teaser great distances, you can approach the turtle or ray, make a super long cast before it dives down, and then work the teaser back to the boat. Any fish associated with the turtle or ray that is looking to feed will follow the teaser, giving the opportunity to sight cast the fish.

Whale sharks are another species that attract cobia, along with other gamefish. On the surface, they provide feeding fish shade and sanctuary from other predatory fish. It's best to approach whale sharks from the side and slightly behind, so they don't spook and swim down. This approach also allows the angler to cast ahead and to one side of the whale shark and then swim the lure or bait down its side and directly into the path of any gamefish that might be hitching a ride.

So keep an eye peeled not just for the species you're targeting, for their colors and shapes, but also for other marine life that may attract, and sometimes even shield the gamefish from view. If you see signs of marine life, look even closer for all those traveling in the same company. SB

CHAPTER 6

Approaching Fish

You're looking for fish, and, in a way, they're looking for you, too. Fish rely on their senses of sight and hearing to avoid predators as well as catch their food, so they rely on those senses to keep them alive. That means you have to take into account how the fish will use those senses to detect you.

Fish don't have eyelids and in most cases their eyes are on the top forward portion of their heads, which means they're often looking forward and upward. Like humans, fish can roll their eyes and move them left or right to get a better view of their peripheral areas of vision, but for objects that are low in the water or are on the edge of their vision, fish have to move their bodies to get a better look. Knowing that fish are generally looking at what is in front of them can give you a better understanding of how to approach a fish in any given situation.

Your best bet is to make a cast to the fish at the greatest distance you feel you have a reasonable opportunity for an accurate cast.

Top, approach fish-holding structure like trees or right, a buoy with a triple-tail, from the best casting angle.

The Angle of Approach

There are times when you want to approach a fish head-on and times to stake out and watch for fish as they approach you head-on. In either case you realize that the fish will now have a good range of vision. The closer the distance between you and the fish the more likely it will detect your presence or any movement. In some cases you can maneuver yourself or your boat into a better approach angle, but if that's not an option, your best bet is to make a cast to the fish at the greatest distance you feel you have a reasonable opportunity for an accurate cast. The farther the fish from you, the better the odds it won't detect your presence and will bite.

The majority of the time you are sight casting

Angler, with boat staked out, waded to position and casts to fish facing upcurrent in a holding spot. A direct approach, on foot or with boat, might have spooked fish.

The sooner you can spot a fish, the quicker you can position yourself at a better angle to have a good cast or multiple casts at that fish.

The angler keeps a lowered profile when presenting to a school of fish approaching with wakes evident in shallow water.

you will be on the move and in control of your angle of approach, so the sooner you can spot a fish, the quicker you can position yourself at a better angle not to be detected and to have a good cast or multiple casts at that fish. What that usually means is approaching fish at an angle on the periphery of its vision or even from behind. That's one of the reasons anglers like to wade upcurrent, because they approach the fish from behind and are less likely to be detected.

Any time you approach fish from the rear you're likely working your way upcurrent or along a bank, bar or offshore rip that is tidally or current directed, which means you are looking for fish that are most likely facing away from you. The key here is to get an idea where the fish are likely to be located, and then place yourself to the side and at a 45- to 90-degree angle from where you think the fish will be.

You never really want to approach a fish from directly behind it, because that limits the angle of your cast. It also increases the odds that your line will cross the fish's back, hit or touch the fish during the cast or retrieve, or make the lure approach

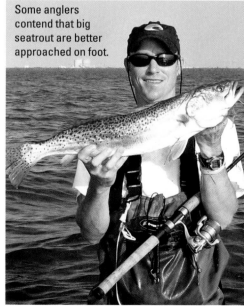

Some anglers contend that big seatrout are better approached on foot.

the fish unnaturally. Remember, baitfish do not attack their predators; they may swim toward them in the current, but once they see a threat they move away at an angle.

CURRENT

The angler on the bow can approach using a trolling motor when fishing solo, or cast from behind the wheel.

Fish Moving Away

When approaching fish from the rear, you want to be off to one side and behind the fish when you make your cast, throwing your lure or bait upcurrent and to one side of the fish so that your retrieve or the natural flow of the current will take the lure or bait into the fish's main area of vision. As the bait gets close to the fish, the angle of your cast will move it toward the side of the fish you are on, which will make the fish think that the prey is making a natural change of course to avoid a predator. That's when you'll get the strike.

Fish Moving In

There are also times when you will fish downcurrent or approach a fish from head-on, and in that instance you also want to be at any angle besides directly head-on, which offers a difficult cast and greater likelihood of detection. If at all possible, you want to be off to one side at a 45- to 90-degree angle to the fish which will give you a considerably better casting angle for presenting a lure or bait in a natural direction of movement.

Position the boat at a 45-degree angle and cast ahead and to the side of the fish. The current will sweep the bait into the strike zone naturally.

CURRENT

ProTip: Sight Casting Spotted Seatrout

Spotted seatrout are one of the toughest species to sight cast, particularly the larger trophy fish in shallow water where they are exceptionally spooky. Their excellent senses of sight and hearing make it difficult for even some of the best anglers to approach within casting range and make the perfect cast required to get these fish to bite.

Look for seatrout in less than two feet of water over mud bottom during sunny days in the middle of the winter, with special attention to shorelines and coves that face southwest, which blocks the easterly breezes and allows the sun to heat the bottom throughout the day. The fish will be sitting dormant on the bottom, and look like logs (cast to anything that looks like a log), and usually in groups of anywhere from three to eight fish.

"The key here is to move slowly down the shorelines while looking for the characteristic shape and size of fish over the dark colored mud," said Capt. Ed Zyak of Jensen Beach, Florida. "Most anglers fish too fast, and end up getting too close to the fish. The fish will look dark brown over the top of the black mud and are usually facing away from shore."

It's imperative that you see the fish from a distance (the longest cast possible), to limit the fish's ability to sense your presence either through sound or movement. If you get close enough to the fish that you can easily determine its shape and size, then the fish will likely see your movements when you make the cast and spook.

"You want to be far enough from the fish that you can just see its outline. Then, get ready and make a super long cast, which will limit the

At low tide on the flats of the Indian River Lagoon—Zyak's home waters—anglers wade for seatrout and snook. Right, Capt. Ed Zyak with gator seatrout.

fish's ability to see your movement," said Zyak. "The cast has to land on the angler's side of the fish's peripheral vision. If it lands past the fish or in front of it, it will probably spook."

Zyak also stresses that the offering has to land silently, because any splash from a bait hitting the water nearby will spook the school. When the offering hits the water, the fish will slowly turn toward the bait and with a single kick of the tail, lash out and strike.

"I sight cast these fish with 10-pound braided line and a 15-pound fluorocarbon leader, which allows me to make a long cast with very little chance the fish will see or detect the line," said Zyak. "In the winter, the diatoms in the water die off and settle to the bottom, so the water will be very clear, and the fish will see you as well as you see

them. The most important thing is to cast to the fish as soon as you see them, and don't wait for one of the fish in the school to see you move or hear your footsteps in the boat."

Capt. Ed Zyak of Jensen Beach, FL is a fulltime fishing guide on the Indian River, and regularly catches seatrout up to 12 pounds. Zyak is considered an authority on sight casting trophy seatrout and targeting everything from snook and redfish to pompano and tarpon on the flats.

The Sound Factor

Just because fish don't have external ears doesn't mean they can't hear. In fact, most fish hear extremely well and because sound travels at a greater distance underwater you need to make sure you limit the noise you make when looking for and approaching fish. Conversely, you can utilize sound to your advantage to attract some gamefish.

One of the fastest ways to alert fish to your presence and shut down a bite is to make a lot of noise, whether you're in the boat or wading. While fish may be accustomed to the sound of boat motors which travels great distances, they aren't used to the clanging of metal, the shutting of hatches or cooler lids, footsteps on a deck or even the loud splashing of water when you walk quickly in the shallows. All of these sounds will put a fish on its guard and move it off in a different direction.

Pay attention to all your movements when on the boat or shore, and start reacting to them. You can easily change your fishing habits so that you close a livewell lid by slowly lowering it to the deck or walk more gingerly on the deck.

Fish are creatures of habit, and over time they learn to associate specific noises with the approach of predators, particularly in areas where there is plenty of fishing pressure. There was a time when an electric trolling motor didn't make tarpon react and the crunch of a graphite pushpole striking coral or rock didn't send schooling bonefish off the flat and into deeper water, but just about any area that sees a lot of angling pressure will have fish reacting to the sounds they learn to associate with fishermen. That is why outboard motors will often put a finning sailfish or cobia down.

As you learn these little adaptations in sound you can use that information to your advantage. For instance, you can still approach tarpon on the beach using your trolling motor, but now you have to run it at a lower power—one that emits less sound, and even turn it off completely when you get into position to make a cast. For bonefish you dip the pole into the bottom lightly as you approach the fish, feeling for the content of the

A redfish feeding exposes its tail, tipping off the angler, who gets off the cast after approaching with a trolling motor to minimize sound.

mud or sand before you push the boat. You now use the trolling motor to get closer to that sailfish or cobia, or shut it down in the path of the fish and wait for it to get closer to the boat before making a cast. In all these instances the angler has adapted or even eliminated the decibel level of noise going into the water.

Anglers can also use sound to their advantage to draw fish into casting range or to attract them to the lure or bait they're offering. A good example of using sound is by throwing lures with rattles in them or adding a rattle chamber to a soft-plastic bait or fly. Rattles mimic the sounds of baitfish schools, shrimp, crawfish and other marine life.

Topwater plugs with spinners or poppers emit a distinct sound much like a splashing or darting

You can change your fishing habits so that you close a livewell lid by slowly lowering it to the deck or walk more gingerly on the deck.

baitfish. That sound helps draw a fish's attention to the lure long before the fish can actually see the offering. Popping or rattling corks used in conjunction with live bait or lures are another way to use sound to attract a fish's attention. A fish approaching might not see it, but with a yank of the rodtip you can send a sound wave similar to an escaping bait that will immediately draw a fish's attention and allow it to see your offering.

Popping corks cast well, provide a mark and make a sound when popped that replicates a feeding fish.

Fly angler strips line to animate fly as migrating tarpon approach across a well-lit flat.

Keep Your Distance

Whenever possible, make the longest cast you can at any fish you spot. Unlike randomly casting a lure or bait where you are arbitrarily searching out a bite from fish you don't see, with sight fishing you are watching the fish and its reactions and are so close to the fish that it can detect your presence and see your movements. You want to put the most distance possible between you and the fish and still make an accurate cast. The farther away you are from a fish the less likely it will hear any sounds you inadvertently make.

Also, the farther you can be from a fish when you make a cast, the better the odds that you will be able to make a second or repeated casts to that fish if your accuracy is off or you don't get the reaction you're looking for. Long casts mean a longer retrieve, so if a fish decides to follow you have a better chance that it will strike before it can see you or detect your presence.

Remaining far away from the fish you're trying to catch will allow you to change the angle as well, and hopefully improve to a more favorable direction and movement of your lure and bait. There are times when you'll spot fish and just have a bad casting angle where you know your line is going to cross the fish's back and spook it—or your bait won't come close enough to the fish for it to see it and strike. But because you're a good distance from the fish you can adjust the angle by moving and repositioning yourself for a better presentation, one that will draw an explosive strike!

Bluewater gamefish are some of the toughest

Rolling tarpon, above, will surface, disappear and often reappear quickly. Best cast will be from as far as possible while maintaining accuracy. Below, tarpon being revived for release.

It's better to get a bait near the fish and hope it will spot your offering than to never make the cast.

fish to approach without spooking, primarily because the environment they live in tends to offer clean, clear water and a depth that allows the fish to see anything approaching from a distance. Fish swimming on the surface such as a tailing sailfish or a dolphin holding under some weeds don't have the advantage of looking up and seeing the silhouette of a boat approaching as a fish that is deeper in the water column might, but they can see movement from a good distance, so they need to be approached slowly from an angle. Because the fish can go down or swim off at any second, as soon as the fish comes within casting range is the time to make the cast. If you wait for the perfect angle and distance, you may have the fish disappear without ever getting off a cast.

So take advantage of the opportunity as it presents itself, even if it isn't the optimum casting angle or distance for an accurate cast. It's better to get a bait near the fish and hope it will spot your offering than to never make the cast.

Sargassum weed above and dolphin below are a classic scenario offshore. It's only a matter of getting the right bait in the water before they're gone.

Slow Down, You Move Too Fast

"If you can see the fish, the fish can see you."

There's wisdom in that old saying, but let's think about it for a moment. Assume for the sake of argument that a big old trout (fresh or salt variety) has its eyes on you. The big question is, how does the fish interpret that visual input?

A lot of the time, you're just another floating or inanimate object in the fish's eyes. But then you move.

Movement is one of the primary ways a fish identifies a potential threat. To avoid getting "busted," you need to make slow, concerted movements at all times, but even more so when approaching fish you're planning to sight cast. The simple sweep of a fishing rod when casting to a fish is a movement that a fish can see and spook from. If you're fly fishing, you may need to make several false casts before you can shoot the fly line, and every time you propel that rod forward and backward there's the possibility that a fish will see that movement.

Making the longest cast possible helps deter that detection by blending the angler into the background so that movements are more closely related to trees or clouds in the wind. As you enter the foreground of the fish's vision, every little movement will be magnified. The closer you get to a fish the slower and more deliberately you should make your movements.

Long, accurate casts at good angles are not always the scenario before you, so do the best with each situation. To make it harder for a fish to detect your movements, bend forward or crouch your body closer to the water. Because fish are constantly looking forward and upward, lowering the angle of your body to the water decreases the chances that they'll see you. Remember that glare on the surface of the water is not just seen when looking down, it's also seen when looking up. From below the surface, the separation between water and air is more mirrorlike, and objects above the water viewed from below are not as well defined. But when that object moves, it's

Casting from ends of the boat, anglers can divvy up and maximize opportunities to prospect along the shoreline they are working.

obvious (suddenly crouching at the last second can be counterproductive for this reason).

Don't forget that your shadow is moving, too. The lower the sun is to the horizon the longer your shadow will cast into the water. Predators like ospreys and eagles cast shadows that move constantly and fish grow up learning that a moving shadow is related to some form of threat, so move slowly and be aware of the location of your shadow. If possible, fish into the sun so your shadow is behind your body, not between you and the fish.

If fishing from land and approaching an area you plan to sight fish, move up to the water slowly, and if possible, use available vegetation or trees to hide your movement. You can hide behind that object, pausing to look for fish. Then if you spot a fish to cast to, you can slowly step away from the object and make the cast. SB

CHAPTER 7

Natural Bait Techniques

O ne of the first things you'll learn when fishing with live baits is that all baits do not cast alike. Some are lighter than others, some are frail and quite a few natural baits are not aerodynamic. They don't cast well at all, particularly not into the wind. These are considerations to make before you ever try to make a cast to a fish you've sighted.

Any time you're fishing live or natural baits you want to consider the size and weight of the baits you're planning to cast because there are options that will improve their castability. At the same time, you still want the bait to have a natural swimming motion so it looks and acts real as it approaches the fish.

In all scenarios, one of the big keys to getting the strike is maneuvering the bait into the fish's strike zone and then keeping it there until the fish sees it.

A snook in its habitat of sand and grass shallows is quick to hit any prey unlucky enough to be visible.

Bait Choice for Casting Accuracy

In some cases, you can use a larger bait to help cast farther. Shrimp and crabs are good examples. When using live shrimp or crabs, the larger the bait, the more it weighs and the better it casts. The size of the shrimp or crab you choose to utilize may be limited by the size of the mouth on the fish you plan to target. Bonefish, for example, have small mouths, which will limit the size of the

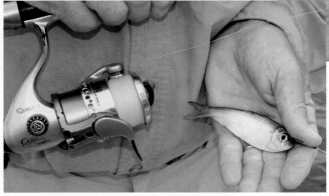

shrimp or crab you can cast. If the bait is too big, the fish won't eat it, or if it does try, it won't get it into its mouth, so you miss the hookset. Tarpon and permit have fairly large mouths which allow an angler to jump up to a more castable size bait. Even when using a larger size shrimp or crab, the fish you're targeting is larger, so you have to use heavier gear, which means you again lose some casting distance.

Top, crabs have been declawed to use as baits. Hooked near the point of the shell, crabs can catch air and fly awkwardly when cast. Bottom, nose-hooked pilchards can be cast accurately but not great distances.

To improve casting distance you can also drop down a size in tackle, going to a lighter rod and thinner braided line, or to a longer rod.

A school of permit's sickle-shaped fins break the surface. A good cast will land close to the fish, ahead of it.

Probably the best way to combat the need for smaller, lighter baits is to add a small piece of lead or splitshot just above the hook. Keep in mind that the additional weight will also create a bit more splash when it enters the water, so you can't cast it as close to the fish as you would with a lighter bait.

Another good option to increase the casting distance of a shrimp or crab is to add a leadhead. The heavier leadheads will limit the movement of the bait. Leadheads come in assorted shapes and sizes from $1/16$ ounce to over one ounce, and you'll want to go with the lightest leadhead that

will give you the casting range you desire.

In a pinch, to improve casting distance you can also drop down a size in tackle, going to a lighter rod and thinner braided line, or go to a longer rod which will improve casting distance but also impact your accuracy. But if you're not getting your bait in front of the fish, you can't get the bite.

When sight fishing with live shiners in fresh water, you can add a splitshot or even put on a weighted cork. The addition of weight will improve the casting distance of the baits, and the weighted cork is a good method for getting better distance without limiting the maneuverability and natural action of the baits.

Some baits, because of their inherent shape and design, don't cast very well. The herring and shad species are examples. The deep, thick bodies of these baitfish make them cast poorly, particularly against the wind. If possible, you can maneuver your boat so that you have a downwind cast at the fish, but that's not always an option. If you have to cast a bait like a shad or herring against the wind, you want to do it with spinning, not baitcasting tackle because as the bait gets caught up in the wind and pauses, the revolving spool of a baitcasting reel will usually backlash, leaving you with a bait in the water and a giant knot on your reel. If a fish does eat the bait, the outcome is usually going to be bad.

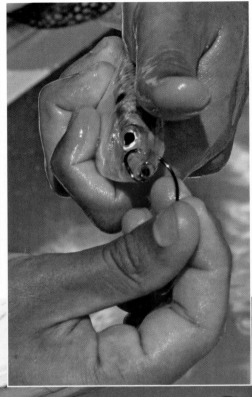

A pilchard nose-hooked will cast better than if hooked just back of dorsal or in the belly. Bottom, with a livewell full of different species, the choice of bait will depend on its castability and on what species are targeted.

If you have different baits in your livewell—a common scenario when offshore fishing—try to pick the most aerodynamic bait to cast first. For instance, if you have threadfin herring, Spanish sardines and blue runners in the livewell and are planning to run-and-gun the weedlines looking for dolphin, you want to use the Spanish sardine, which is long, heavy and casts like a bullet. Next go to the blue runner which is not very aerodynamic but is a heavier bait, and finally the threadfins.

Leading Fish with Casts

There's an old adage among fishing guides that goes, "Food does not fall out of the sky," which means predatory fish are not used to their meals landing on top of their heads. In most cases, they

Leading a fish with a cast and letting the live bait's action draw the fish nearer can be better than getting too close to that fish.

either have to chase down their food or have the current or tide sweep it in their direction.

In customary sight fishing conditions with clear water, fish will have a better view of what is in front of them. The majority of times you cast at fish, you don't want the fish to see the bait hit the water. If a fish sees your bait land, it will know that is not the normal action of that bait, and will instantly be on its guard. (Ocean species such as dolphin and tunas are an exception—they may chase your bait as it arcs through the air, grabbing it as soon as it lands, probably an adaptation from foraging on flyingfish.)

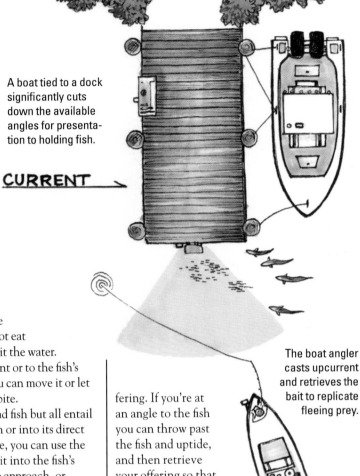

A boat tied to a dock significantly cuts down the available angles for presentation to holding fish.

CURRENT

The boat angler casts upcurrent and retrieves the bait to replicate fleeing prey.

In stream trout fishing, you want your offering to land above the fish's normal field of vision and then have the current bring the bait down to the fish. If you cast close to the trout, it knows something is wrong and won't eat. The same goes with tarpon, which will not eat a shrimp or crab if they see it hit the water. But cast that bait farther in front or to the fish's peripheral vision, and then you can move it or let the fish approach it to get the bite.

There are lots of ways to lead fish but all entail making a cast ahead of the fish or into its direct path of movement. From there, you can use the tide or current to bring the bait into the fish's strike zone, wait for the fish to approach, or retrieve the bait toward the fish. All are very effective, but it all starts with the perfect cast.

Say you're wading a sandbar for striped bass or redfish. The fish are feeding into the tide and moving in a specific direction. You know that tide will carry scent along with it, so you can cast a natural bait well uptide of the fish and wait for the fish's sense of smell to locate it or for the fish to move forward, into the area of the of-

fering. If you're at an angle to the fish you can throw past the fish and uptide, and then retrieve your offering so that the tide swings it in front of the fish and into their strike zone. Or you can simply make a cast just in front of the fish and above their field of vision, let the bait sit until the school works its way forward to where the bait is, then move it to let the fish see it and wait for the strike.

Another common scenario greets bridge fishermen who are looking down into the water and regularly see fish sitting upcurrent of the bridge along a shadowline facing into the tide. Positioning behind and to one side of the fish you remain undetected and can cast upcurrent of where the fish is holding, above its field of vision, and let the bait sweep toward the fish with the tide. Casting

Casting past the fish prevents the fish from seeing the offering hit the water, and you can then maneuever it into the fish's field of vision like a normal food item.

Predators wait for baits disoriented in the wash against rocks to strike. Anglers need to put their casts into that action, often right against rocks.

past the fish at an angle allows you to reel or work the offering into the fish's strike zone.

When approaching a stationary fish in no current head-on, you can change the angle to more of a 45- to 90-degree angle and then cast beyond the fish and retrieve the bait into the fish's strike zone, or you can cast ahead and directly in line with the fish, and wait for it to move closer to you before moving the bait. With live baits, the bait will sometimes swim in the direction of the fish and into its strike zone. The drawback to the second scenario is that the fish usually has to move closer to you and is more likely to detect your presence, so after you make the cast, crouch your body forward to decrease your profile and remain still until the fish approaches the bait. Then work the offering with slow, deliberate movements.

Bluewater fish tend to be more aggressive and opportunistic feeders than inshore saltwater or freshwater gamefish. A dolphin, sailfish or wahoo must find its food in miles of open ocean, and when it does it must take advantage of every opportunity to feed because it doesn't know when it will encounter the next meal. Because these fish

are more aggressive you can usually place your cast closer to the fish without spooking it, but you still have to put the bait into the fish's field of vision. If you cast behind or to the side of a sailfish it will likely keep moving forward and never see the bait. But place that bait out ahead of the moving fish, and the clear ocean water will allow that fish to see the bait from a great distance and take advantage of the easy meal.

A bass under a dock may be stationary or moving, but in either scenario you want to make a cast past the dock and the fish and retrieve your bait back into the strike zone. Casting past the fish prevents the fish from seeing the offering hit the water, and you can then maneuver it into the fish's field of vision just as a normal food item would come into the strike zone. You'll know if the fish is interested by watching its posture.

In all these scenarios one of the big keys to getting the strike is maneuvering the bait into the fish's strike zone and then keeping it there until the fish sees the bait. Most of the time, the fish will immediately charge the bait and eat it, but there are other times when the bait has to remain in the strike zone for a prolonged period until it enrages the fish or the fish can't take it any longer and strikes.

Keeping Your Bait in the Strike Zone

The longer you can keep a bait in the strike zone the greater the odds that the fish will eat it. It's that simple. Put food in front of a wild animal and if it believes that it is real and poses no threat, it will exhibit its natural instincts which are to consume the easy meal. But keeping a bait in the strike zone isn't always easy.

Moving tides and current, moving fish and live, swimming baits are all factors that need to be considered along with the depth of the water, angle of the retrieve and what it takes to make the bait intercept the fish's path. Processing all these considerations will come naturally as you gain experience, and eventually they become natural actions that require little thinking.

Figuring out moving tides or currents is probably the most common scenario in the presentation of natural baits, because fresh and saltwater gamefish regularly depend on moving water to bring their food to them. In a trout stream, a worm will flow past a fish in the current rather quickly, but you can slow that drift or even stop the worm on the bottom by adding a splitshot ahead of the worm,

casting upstream of the fish and using the rod to bounce the bait into the strike zone. Once the worm gets into the fish's visual strike zone, you can lower the rodtip, effectively allowing the weight to hold the worm in place until the fish opts to move forward and consume the morsel.

A similar scenario can be utilized when sight fishing bonefish on a flat using live shrimp in a moving current. You can put a splitshot on the line ahead of the shrimp (either close to the hook or up to 18 inches away), take advantage of the extra weight to increase the casting distance, and then maneuver the shrimp in the path of an approaching bonefish. Then stop the retrieve, let the bait settle to the bottom and let the natural senses of sight and smell lead the bonefish to the shrimp.

For stationary fish you can add a splitshot or weight ahead of a live natural bait, then cast past the stationary fish and outside its peripheral vision, and then reel the bait toward the fish and to the edge of its strike zone. Be sure not to reel the bait right to the fish's nose, as it's not natural for a food item to attack or approach its prey. Just get the bait into the strike zone (usually you'll notice a change in posture with the fish when it sees the bait), then

Bottom Bumpers

Top, a tail-weighted shrimp on the retrieve will hop along the bottom—as if swimming backward naturally—to entice bites. A small crab hooked for permit will dive to the bottom and try to dig in, but not before permit in the vicinity see it and pursue it—or not.

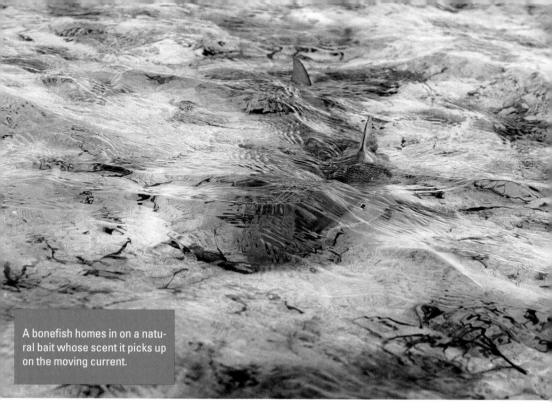

A bonefish homes in on a natural bait whose scent it picks up on the moving current.

The longer you keep a bait in front of your target, the better your odds.

stop it, allowing the weight to hold the bait in place and keep it from swimming or moving off.

When sight casting to moving fish like a cobia swimming on the surface or a redfish feeding along a shoreline, the key is to make a cast past the fish and then use the reel to position the bait in the fish's path. If you're in a boat and can place yourself ahead of the fish, you can use the motor, or even better, the trolling motor which is silent, to keep the same distance between you and the fish while at the same time pulling the bait forward and keeping it in front of the gamefish.

There are times when that redfish will be in a bit deeper water yet still visible and a target for the sight-casting angler. The inherent problem with sight casting to fish in deeper water is that live baits may swim to the surface and out of the strike zone. In this case, you can add some extra weight either in the form of a splitshot, sinker or jighead. With live shrimp, adding a jighead will allow the bait to remain live and natural acting while it's bounced along the bottom and into the fish's field of vision

where it can be paused until the fish decides to eat.

Jigheads and other weights can also be used to make a bait exhibit its natural escape actions as with a live crab, one of the best baits for permit. Crabs swimming on the flats will dive to the bottom and burrow in the sand when exposed to danger, but a hooked crab may find that difficult because of the friction of the line in the water. To make a crab dive, add a jighead to the offering, hooking the crab in the point of the shell with the jighead just as you would a bare hook. When cast in front of an approaching permit, the crab can be reeled along the surface until it's in front of the fish, then allowed to sink to the bottom just as a crab that feels threatened would do. The permit in turn, will tip up, follow the crab down and eat.

The longer you can keep a bait in front of your target and in its strike zone, the better the odds of getting that fish to eat. There are times when a fish doesn't really need to feed, but eventually will eat just because an opportunity for an easy meal presents itself.

Left, chunking chum and bait. Chumbuoy for remote release. Lower, surface chum-bag and weighted bag for bottom.

Using Scent to Your Advantage

Besides looking and acting like the "real deal," natural baits will add scent to the water, and for many fish their sense of smell is a major means of locating food. Redfish and bonefish are good examples. Both species regularly rely on their sense of smell to find shrimp and other baits on the flats.

Shrimp are one of the most commonly used baits for saltwater inshore and flats fishing, but a whole live shrimp doesn't put a lot of scent into the water. Change that by pinching the tail off a shrimp, which exposes the crustacean inside the protective outer shell and releases scent into the water that fish can smell from great distances.

Any time you're wanting to utilize scent to help a fish locate a bait you want to place that bait either upcurrent of the fish or directly in the fish's path. Fish like bonefish regularly feed into the current just so they can utilize their strong sense of smell to locate their food, and putting that shrimp upcurrent of the bonefish will greatly increase the odds of that fish locating the bait.

A similar scenario presents itself in blue water where cobia regularly swim either with or against the current when on the surface. One of the best cobia baits is a whole, dead squid because it emits a lot of scent. When cobia are feeding into the current you can cast that squid ahead of the approaching fish and let the normal movement of the water allow the scent to be swept into the path of the fish. If the fish is moving with the current, you can cast the bait past the fish and reel it ahead of the fish and across its path, where it will then swim into the path of the scent and can follow that scent directly to the squid.

When fishing with live baits you can use a pair of scissors to trim their tail, make a cut in the tail or trim the dorsal fin to help emit scent into the water. This will also inhibit the bait's natural movements and limit its ability to escape its predators. Just be sure to make small cuts or trims, because while a large cut will release scent into the water it will also cause harm to the bait-fish, and if you cause enough trauma to the bait, it will eventually die. That's fine for targeting some species but gamefish that prefer lively baits will turn away from the dead offering.

Not all sight fishing opportunities offer

current or tide to aid in directing the scent of your bait to the fish. The scenario of a gamefish swimming along a shoreline, such as a striped bass or redfish in a bay system, still allows you to use scent to your advantage. In this case, you want to cast ahead and past the moving fish then reel the bait into its path before allowing it to sit there. A shrimp, clam or chunk of baitfish will put a lot of smell into the water, and that smell will be in a straight line from where the bait hit the water to where it was stopped so that a fish that wavers off course slightly will still swim into the scent trail. Once that striper or redfish intercepts the scent trail it can follow directly to the bait. The closer it gets to the bait, the stronger the scent until the fish locates the bait and eats. Never hesitate to pinch that tail off your natural bait to let its scent spread. SB

Sheepshead's teeth, top, are made for grinding shell. Anglers, left, chum the fish by scraping oysters off pilings.

CHAPTER 8

Artificial Bait Techniques

Any time you're looking to sight cast to fish using artificials, the weight of your lure or fly is going to play a major factor in how you go about making a cast. The weight of your lure will provide advantages and disadvantages, and you need to know these factors before you make the cast. Increased weight often improves casting distance to a point, but that weight also means the lure will land loudly in the water, which can spook fish. The more the lure weighs, the farther it will cast until the point at which it is so heavy that it overloads the rod and you compromise distance or even risk breaking the rod or lure.

The heavier the lure, the more sound and splash it makes when it hits water, and when fish are in the shallows, they're hyper-aware of threatening sounds.

Anglers in a back-
country mangrove
channel work a chug-
ger to attract bites.
Right, a seatrout
crushes a topwater.

Artificial Lure Castability

As you work the lure onto the bed, stop it on top of the bed and shake your rodtip. The movement will activate the lure.

For many baits, like jigs or soft-plastics where you can add a jighead, the amount of weight you choose not only determines how far the lure will cast, but also how deep it will swim. You can control that depth for the most part by varying the speed of the retrieve. In that case, you want to err on the side of the bait being lighter. Slowing down the lure to make it sink farther is better because it keeps the lure in the strike zone longer. Having to speed up a lure to keep it at a specific depth moves it through the strike zone faster, which limits the amount of time a fish has to react to the bait.

As with fishing live bait, the longer the cast you can make the better the chance the fish will not detect your presence and the greater the odds of getting a bite. A spawning bass guarding its bed will remain on top of the bed to prevent predators such as bluegill and salamanders from eating its eggs. If that fish detects your presence it will move off the bed but remain nearby until the threat moves off, then move right back into position to guard its eggs.

Knowing this, if you come upon a bass on a bed you immediately want to back up and make the longest cast possible. That decreases the odds that the fish will see any movement or detect your presence and increase the odds that the bass will hit your lure. Make a long cast past the spawning bed and then work your lure (either a worm, salamander or other creature-type bait) over to the bed so that the fish sees the threat approaching. Your lure only poses a threat to the bass while it is on the bed, so as you work the lure

onto the bed, stop it on top of the bed and shake your rodtip. The movement will give the lure action while allowing it to remain in place. The fish will see that as a threat to its eggs and pounce on

The screw-lock sinker, above. Below, from top, toothpick to snug sinker, pick at back of weight, knot to lock, and rubberband stop.

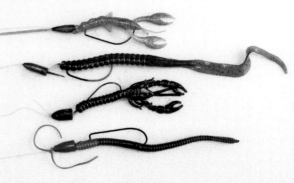

the offering. In this instance you'll want to add enough weight to your lure so it casts well and also sinks all the way to the bottom, so you can crawl it along and onto the spawning bed.

A distance cast hits its target, top. Below, a chunky bass pulled from the hydrilla at a Florida reservoir.

Take another case of the same principle from the saltwater world. Let's say you're casting a jig for pompano while wading down a sandbar. Pompano are sight feeders that look for shrimp and crabs scurrying in the sand. Because you are wading, you present a low profile, which will enable you to get close to the fish without detection, but you still want to use a lure that's heavy enough so that it will bounce and create little puffs of sand every time it hits the bottom. The pompano will find the lure by the sand it kicks up.

Weight can also be a hindrance when fishing lures. When casting at bonefish on a flat, snook along a shoreline or big seatrout in shallow water, the loud sound of a heavy lure hitting the water will send these fish heading for cover. The heavier the lure, the more sound and splash it makes when it hits the water. When fish are in the shallows they are hyper-aware of sounds that they feel are unnatural or might indicate a threat.

To minimize the ill effects of this, you can do one of two things: make longer casts past the fish so that they don't hear the lure hitting the water, or go to a lighter lure. Making a longer cast will place the lure outside the fish's normal range of hearing, so it's less likely to react to the sound of the lure hitting the water. Then you can work the lure in front of the fish. The drawback to this is that the longer the cast, the less accurate, which is why switching to a lighter lure is usually better.

Pompano chase down the jig, with stinger, from some distance. Below, a box of pomp jigs in one angler's favorite colors.

Lure color should be one of your first decisions. Some fish and some locations favor particular colors.

Yes, Lure Color Makes a Difference

For years, anglers have wondered if fish see colors. With the advent of electron microscopes, ichthyologists have been able to identify a complex system of rods and cones in fish eyes that resemble the sensory organs in human eyes. These structures indeed help fish to see colors. There are specific situations where limited light does control the amount of color a fish can see, but even in those circumstances fish will usually see silhouettes or shadows of specific colors better than others.

That being said, lure color should be one of your first decisions when rigging up to sight cast. Some fish and some locations are prone to favor particular colors. A lot has to do with the seasonality of the natural forage in the area. If it's fall in Georgia, Louisiana or Texas and the shrimp are coming out of the marsh, then shrimp are likely the main diet of seatrout and redfish. So if you're looking to sight cast these fish with lures, picking a shrimp lure that is light brown, pink or green would be the best choice, dependent on the species and coloration of the shrimp in your area.

The same goes for bass feeding on shad in a clear lake. Most shad are black and silver, green and silver or blue and silver, depending on the visibility of the water in the lake and the species of shad. Throwing an orange crankbait that resembles a crawfish is counterproductive if the bass are feeding on shad.

Some fish see bright colors better than others, which is why pink, chartreuse and orange are great colors to use when sight casting pompano over sand. Shrimp will also exhibit these hues when over sand, and they're a main dietary item for pompano.

Baitfish offshore typically have blue or green colored backs and silver sides depending on the water they're in. Nature has provided those

The protective encasement of a redfish's eye also draws in light to amplify the fish's vision.

A snook's eye, near top of its head, is positioned to look forward and upward for prey and predator.

Successful imitations mimic the colors of local natural baits. Below, redfish with a life-like Gulp! shrimp.

colorations to help these baitfish blend in to their environments, thus improving their chances for survival. You want to make your baits look the most natural at all times. When trying to mimic a natural prey item, pay attention to all the

a crab from above will see it as green, but if crabs are floating on the surface and the fish sees it from below, the underside of the bait is white, so an all green crab won't catch the fish feeding on the surface. You need to have a green back and white underbelly on your bait.

When you're throwing a lure, you want to think about not only the colorations of the bait you're trying to mimic, but also how water can alter those colors. A mullet in clear water is very light, almost grey colored, but in tannin-stained water, it's black. The silver sides of a mullet in clear water shine silver, but in dark, tannic, acid-stained water they shine gold. You would throw a grey or chartreuse backed lure with silver sides in clear water, and a black back lure with gold sides in tannic-colored water.

Many fish are very color specific based on their regions. Consider black bass. In Florida, the Junebug (black grape/green glitter) colored worm is king. In Texas, it's red shad color. In North Carolina, the purple worm is tops. Striped bass like chartreuse, as do cobia. Snook and seatrout love dark green and silver, while redfish prefer gold. Muskies like bright colors. Smallmouth bass like dark colors.

Colors do matter. It's up to you to discern the favored colors for the gamefish you're targeting,

Top, an array of artificial shrimp in colors for dark and light water conditions. Below, when retrieved, jointed swimbaits not only mimic baits' colors but they move with snake-like action to prompt strikes from nearby gamefish.

colorations and hues. Crabs for instance, can be red, blue, green or brown. While an angler might see the green back of a blue crab and choose a green lure to mimic the bait, that may not always be the better choice of colors. A fish approaching

the colors of their natural forage and how those colors are impacted by water clarity and their surroundings. All these factors change regularly. That's why anglers have so many different colored lures and flies.

A weedless hook is a stealthy way to rig life-like scented baits—like this shrimp and jerk shad—for surface and shallow presentations. The large containers keep the baits well-dosed with scented liquid.

Nature has provided those colorations to help baitfish blend in to their environments. You want to make your baits look the most natural at all times. You can draw interest in them by using scented imitations.

Sight Fishing with Topwater Lures

One of the most rewarding sight casting opportunities is to catch a fish on a topwater lure. Besides stalking and finding fish, getting them to eat is the toughest part, and when you can trick a fish into eating a fake bait on the surface, the bite just doesn't get more exciting. Just about any angler will choose an explosive topwater strike over just about any other option in fishing.

To get fish to eat a topwater bait you need to find them feeding in an area where the forage swims on the surface. That may be time, location or seasonally determined depending on the fish and baits you're chasing, but when it does come together, the visual aspect of working a bait and seeing the fish react and eat are the epitome of sight fishing.

Time of day seems to play a consistent role in determining whether fish feed on the surface. Early mornings are when you'll often find snook and big jack crevalle feeding along seawalls, as they use the low light conditions to ambush mullet and other baitfish and pin them to the cement. These fish are most active because the early morning is the coolest period of the day, and the low light affords these fish an advantage when stalking their prey. This is the time to throw a topwater lure parallel to the seawall and work it down the structure.

For offshore fish like cobia and amberjack, location may play a larger role. Finding these fish is key, and getting them to eat on the surface is more about their attitude at the moment. Cobia and amberjack like to hang around reefs and wrecks, so that's where the game often starts. Time of day may also play a factor, as amberjacks like to swim near the surface at dawn, as do cobia.

Seasonal changes may also affect the topwater bite. Shrimp and crabs that are carried out inlets or marshes with the tides have annual runs that take place during specific times of the year. Permit

Big jack crevalle zeroes in on a topwater plug with a fast retrieve. Hookless, the plug acts as a teaser.

A variety of hard-body prop lures for producing sound and splash.

and tarpon feeding on crabs around a Florida Keys bridge will be there in May, June and July, while a tarpon feeding on shrimp at night in Miami's Government Cut about 90 miles away will be that February through April.

Bait runs are a huge factor in gamefish movements, and also how aggressively they stalk and eat their prey. In Florida waters during the fall, massive schools of mullet push south along the Atlantic Coast, with inshore and nearshore gamefish completely focused on eating them.

How you work a lure may inspire a fish to eat or flee. Remember that prey does not attack a predator, so working your lure directly toward a fish is counterproductive. Instead, cast upcurrent and at an angle so the bait flows to the fish naturally and in an evasive manner.

There's a cool nighttime snook bite that takes place in Florida during the fall months when the finger mullet are migrating through the inshore waters in schools. Snook position themselves on the dark side of a shadowline facing upcurrent

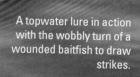

A topwater lure in action with the wobbly turn of a wounded baitfish to draw strikes.

In the heart of snook country in East Central Florida, an angler works the light and shadow-lines under the Roosevelt Bride. Below, beneath the same bridge, the angler directs his cast to the ambush point at the corner of a bridge base. Snook use the structure, light and currents to ambush prey.

and wait for the mullet to move from where the overhead light from the bridges or docks meets the dark shadow of the structure. Where light meets dark and the hapless mullet lose their vision (as their eyes adjust to the darkness), the snook strike.

That ambush point isn't uncommon when sight fishing gamefish like snook around bridges and docks. What is odd is that the fish prefer the topwater lure to pause in the light and drift, not swim into the darkness just as the mullet do. If you work or swim a topwater lure from light to dark you get about a third the bites you would get if you paused the lure just before the shadowline and let it drift into the darkness.

Topwater lures are a rewarding way to get a bite, but if the fish are feeding on baits below the surface, you might go to a subsurface bait. After all, it's only cool to watch if you get the bite.

Where light meets dark and the mullet lose their vision (as their eyes adjust to the darkness) the snook strike.

A bright light on an old dock is a good start to finding fish at night. To the left of the dock piling, the snook's form is visible where it waits to feed.

Sight Fishing with Subsurface Baits

Most of the time you see fish sitting below the surface they are feeding on baits that are not on the surface. There

Neutral buoyancy baits like jerkbaits and hard plastics allow an angler to give the lure action as it moves into the zone.

Plastic swimbaits put on jigheads can be retrieved subsurface.

are times when the fish are on the surface and still want a subsurface bait.

The term subsurface covers a lot of the artificial lure spectrum, from hard-body lures that dive, sink or swim below the surface to soft-plastics with a weighted jighead. These lures mimic baits that thrive below the surface, and while you don't get those explosive topwater bites that knock a giant hole in the water, you can usually see the fish react to and eat the lure, which makes fishing these baits just as rewarding.

When it comes to sight fishing with subsurface lures you'll find that there are many dif-ferent presentations you can utilize depending on the lures you are throwing. Jigs for instance, allow the angler to bounce the lure off the bottom, swim it at middepth, or even retrieve the lure so that it rises and falls throughout the water column. Each lure has specific character-istics that determine how it should be fished to best mimic the bait you're trying to represent.

Soft-plastic baits are commonly used with weights, whether that's a tungsten bullet weight ahead of a spring lizard for bass or a leadhead in conjunction with a worm, jerkbait or shad tail. In all these in-stances, you can fish the bait fast, slow or with long pauses depending on how the fish react.

Let's look at snook sitting along a shoreline for example. If you're fishing a boot-tailed grub with a leadhead you want to cast past the fish, and reel the bait so it swims into the strike zone but to one side of the fish. Now

Naturalistic plastics can be used subsurface and allowed to sink to the bottom. Mark Nichols of D.O.A. Lures fights a seatrout. The shrimp lure slid up the line after the fish was hooked.

you can reel it relatively fast with small twitches of the rodtip so that the bait swims high in the water column and past the snook. Or you can lift the rod and then let the bait fall as you gather the slack so that it moves up and down in the water column. You might decide to cast past the fish, let the bait sink all the way to the bottom, and then swim or hop it along the sand, like a sandperch or pinfish. Lastly, you can swim the bait high in the water column until it's in the fish's strike zone, then let it fall to the bottom and hop it along slowly like an injured baitfish.

All these retrieves are effective ways to draw a strike, but how the fish reacts to each individual retrieve will determine your actions. If the fish shows interest in one retrieve, then a similar action with a cast closer or to one side of the fish might be the way to get a strike. If the fish doesn't react to a specific retrieve, don't repeat it. Change things and find the action that makes the fish hit.

Neutral buoyancy baits like jerkbaits and hard plastic crankbaits allow an angler to give the lure action as it comes into the fish's strike zone. Pause the lure in the zone, giving the predator more time to decide to lunge forward and grab the bait. Unweighted jerkbaits (that sink when paused) or sinking hard baits can be fished with a twitch-pause, twitch-pause routine with a one- to two-second pause between twitches. Fish usually strike when the lure is paused in the strike zone.

Subsurface hard baits are a great option when fishing for tarpon around bridges, in an inlet or in moving current. Usually the tarpon are suspended at a specific depth just below the surface, and if you can spot the fish holding in the current you can then choose a lure that swims at that depth and work it into the fish's strike zone.

The same goes for peacock bass holding in

a current near a bridge or guarding a spawning bed along a lakeside shoreline. A sinking crankbait worked past the nose of the fish and in its strike zone will likely draw a reactionary strike even if the fish isn't hungry, whereas a surface bait likely won't even draw a reaction from these normally aggressive gamefish.

Not all sight fishing requires spotting a fish holding in current or working along at a specific depth. Schooling fish like striped bass and bluefish will rise to the surface in big schools as

Subsurface hard plastics and spoons can be animated with a wide range of retrieve styles to entice bites.

they feed or "blitz" baitfish. When you see this feeding frenzy taking place, you can quickly react and cast into the fray with just about any lure that resembles their prey. When the school goes down, you might only see the dark color of the back of the fish, which looks like a half acre of shadow as the school moves along below the surface. Leading the fish with a subsurface bait that swims at the same depth as the school will assure a bite.

Fish hold in specific depths for a reason. That may be for comfort, as they look for deeper water in the middle of the day's heat, but most often fish hold at specific depths because that is where the food supply is. Use lures to target those fish by working the baits into their strike zones.

Fly Fishing Techniques

Flies come in a wide variety of patterns, each designed to mimic specific forage items. There are unweighted, weighted, diving, sinking and floating flies. Each has a specific purpose. Knowing what bait that fly is designed to mimic and doing your best to make the fly act like the real deal is what will get you strikes.

One of the best assets with unweighted or neutral buoyancy flies is that they can be worked with a natural action in front of the fish and then paused in the strike zone for prolonged periods, allowing the fish more time to decide to eat. Some gamefish are even more prone to eating a fly than most lures or even some natural baits because of this factor. Bonefish, tarpon, bass, ladyfish, redfish, carp and muskellunge are all good examples.

Surface flies come in many configurations. Poppers and floating deerhair "plugs" splash and make a lot of noise, often mimicking the sound of panicked baitfish or a bait swimming along on the surface. Along with the natural action of the components of the fly, you get the action the angler imparts on the lure plus the sound the lure makes as it moves along. Traditional dry flies for freshwater trout—the hackled Adams, Royal Coachman, Cahills and kin—are primarily used as passive attractors. No stripping is required, though sometimes a little pull may elicit a strike.

Retrieves for surface flies vary with the patterns and the fish you're targeting. For instance a popping bug for bass, bluegill or other freshwater

Top, deerhair bugs for largemouth bass and saltwater fishing, and lower, a box of nymphs for drifting down riffles and runs in stream trout fishing.

gamefish is usually worked with long pauses between "pops," so that the lure looks more like a frog or injured baitfish. That same popper in a larger size thrown at giant jack crevalle or cobia is worked back to the boat with steady pops and no pause, forcing the fast-pursuing fish to pounce on the fly to catch it.

There are times when unweighted flies are a benefit even though they're designed to sink just below the surface during the retrieve. Not only do these fly patterns swim just below the surface like a juvenile mullet, pinfish or pilchard, but because the fly lacks weight it lands on the water quietly so that it is less likely to spook a wary fish.

This is a great option when sight casting trophy spotted seatrout in the shallows. Seatrout have incredible vision and hearing, so a weighted fly that lands with an audible "plop" will put the fish on their guard and get a denial every time. But a fly that lands silently on the fish's peripheral vision can be paused in place, allowing the fish to notice the fly, turn and lunge out and eat it.

Sinking flies, much like subsurface lures, are designed to work at a specific depth in the water column. Weighted patterns can be designed to sink, crawl along the bottom or swim at a specific depth depending on the bait they mimic. Permit crabs are a good example of the different functions of a sinking fly. In nature, when a crab swimming along on the surface encounters a permit or bonefish in shallow water it dives for the bottom and tries to bury itself in the sand. Permit crabs are weighted and designed so that they can be worked on the surface by stripping the line to present the crab in front of the permit. Then the stripping action is stopped or paused to allow the crab to sink to the bottom like a crab diving. When a permit sees the crab diving, it tips up and pounds the fly.

A very popular streamer pattern for both fresh- and saltwater applications is the Clouser Deep Minnow, which resembles a jig in form and function. The Clouser Minnow is worked into a fish's strike zone at a specific depth, and then either bounced, swam or paused until it elicits a strike. Heavy Clousers can be constantly retrieved at a specific depth dependent on the amount of weight and speed of the retrieve, allowing the fly to swim at a constant depth much like a baitfish. Variations on the theme are made with an array of similar weighted fly patterns.

There are smaller or larger crawfish flies designed for bass and carp that are crawled along the bottom with little hops. Cast in the direct path of oncoming fish and moved at a specific pace, the predator tracks them down. Nymphs used in trout streams are allowed to drift naturally. Every fly or lure has a specific purpose and it's up to the angler to determine which scenarios will allow that lure or fly to draw a strike. SB

Bonefish before release on a tropical flat, top, is one of the most prized sport catches on fly the world over. Right, Capt. Mike Conner casts a fly to entice a bite in skinny water.

CHAPTER 9

Reading Fish

T he better you get at seeking out and finding fish by sight, the more experience you have with the different actions and reactions of your favored species. As you approach a fish and then work hard to sight cast and catch that fish, you will begin to notice its little changes in body postures and actions that will allow you to "read" the fish—to get to know it so well that you can anticipate its next moves.

Over time, you'll develop a kind of sixth sense of when you need to back off, be more aggressive or make another cast. You'll know the course of action you need to take to get the fish to eat the bait whether it wants to or not. That knowledge of a variety of species, along with adept use of a variety of casting, spinning and flyfishing tackle, is a mark of the accomplished angler.

The posture of a fish will let you know when you are about to get a bite. Tarpon are thrilling to watch as they flare their pectoral fins and hump their bodies.

A tarpon hooked and
held by a fly—and mo-
mentarily calm— makes
a prized catch for a sight
fishing angler.

Postures

Each fish species displays consistent reactions to threats and excitement, and the better you focus on watching fish closely and then reacting to their postures, the better you'll get at sight fishing. Sailfish for instance, will light up and change colors when excited or feeding. When you see a fish light up, you know it's having a positive reaction to your offering.

Over time, you'll see that fish strike a lot of different postures that, if read properly, will help clue you in to their mood. Let's say you're sight casting to trout in a stream and watching a fish as it reacts to stoneflies landing on the water to lay eggs. As the big flies are swept into the fish's

When a tarpon "humps up," you pretty much know that the bite is imminent.

field of vision, it moves to a point downstream where it can easily intercept a meal.

When you throw your fly upstream of that fish, it moves into position but when the fly gets close, it doesn't eat. You know the fly has evoked a positive reaction from that fish, but something is keeping it from taking the bug as it gets closer. Likely there is something wrong or weird about the fly,

In this instance you want to back off the fish and change the angle of approach. Watch the fish closely from a distance and wait for it to take on a more relaxed posture or a feeding posture before making the longest cast possible. Often, these changes will elicit the strike.

Off a saltwater beach, spawning-size jack crevalle swimming in a counter-clockwise circle will reveal their mood by moving up or down in the water column and finning, flashing and generally swimming steadily in a circle on the surface. When those fish feel threatened, they'll drop a bit in the water column where their fins don't protrude from the water, or will break off from the circle and move as a line away from the approaching angler. In this case, you want to back off the school and wait for it to calm down, circle up and start swimming on the surface again before making a cast.

A juvenile tarpon waits patiently until the baitfish moving along the mangroves make the mistake of straying too far from the banks.

Many times, the posture of a fish will let you know when you are about to get a bite. Tarpon are thrilling to watch, as the fish flare their pectoral fins and hump their bodies when pursuing a fly or bait. When a tarpon "humps up," you pretty much know the bite is imminent. The classic quiver of a bonefish tail as it accelerates to take a fly also comes to mind.

The thing you want to remember about fish postures is that they are one more indicator as to what the fish might be experiencing and how it is going to react to your offering. If you see a negative posture, with the fish tensing its body, twisting away or even with no change in its posture, it likely isn't going to chase your bait. When you see that positive posture like a spreading of the pectoral fins (everything from sailfish to redfish to brook trout do this), the arching of its body, turning rapidly toward the bait or even simply going from still to a slow but steady swim in the direction of your offering, you can keep your eyes on that reaction all the way until the fish strikes. That anticipation of the fish's action and the confirmation of it by sight adds to the sport's enjoyment.

or the fish is seeing the leader. It might mean the fly is tangled, the coloration is a bit off from the natural stoneflies or that the size is wrong. Or it can mean the tippet is too heavy and the fish is seeing it just before it eats. Or the fly is being pulled unnaturally against the current. Watching the posture of the fish over several casts will give you an idea of what is taking place and a simple change will get the fish to bite.

There are times when you'll see fish change postures from a comfortable position to one on its guard. If that fish hasn't moved off, it likely detects your presence but isn't sure where you are. It still won't eat until it relaxes.

Watching Actions and Reactions

Fish are finicky, and what works one day may not be what they want the next day, or even the next cast. Watch the fish closely for those reactions that tell you a fish is interested, and then duplicate or improve on that action. If the fish are disinterested or turn away, you know to try something different to get the bite.

Cobia are a great example. Casting and watching their reactions to initial presentations often leads to a solid hookup. There are days when you'll encounter surface-swimming cobia that eat everything you throw their way. Then there are those days when they seem like the pickiest fish in the ocean.

Cobia love the color chartreuse, so much so that a large percentage of anglers who sight cast cobia leave the inlet with at least one rod rigged with a chartreuse jig or soft-plastic swimbait. But I've seen times when cobia will not even react to a well-cast chartreuse jig, and then changed to a chartreuse swimbait, and still had no reaction. I've then changed to a chartreuse surface plug with the same results. Then someone on the boat throws an orange jig and the fish climb over the backs of each other to get to the lure.

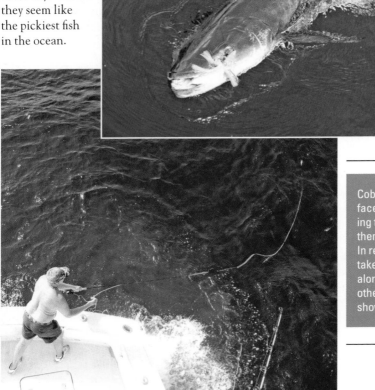

Cobia often cruise on the surface and make top sight fishing targets. Favorite lures for them are bucktail jigs, above. In recent years, anglers have taken to fly fishing for cobia along the Gulf Coast, left, and other locales where the fish show on or near the surface.

Three cobia in hot pursuit of a jig in clear water—a great moment to witness from behind the rod.

Sometimes it's as simple as changing baits. Other times you want to speed up or slow down the retrieve. Bass fishermen sight casting to fish in the shallows can watch the fish closely to see what the fish like, then duplicate that same action or retrieve every time they encounter a fish in the same situation. They call it patterning the fish, and it follows the theory that whatever little reaction draws the bite from one fish should draw the same action or bite from others.

In clear waters, sighted bass can be patterned and that action replicated in a similar scenario. Top right, bass on a D.O.A. Big Fish Lure.

ProTip: Sight Casting Bedding Bass

Let a bigger bait do the work, then plop the smaller bait in front of the fish.

One of the most common mistakes when sight fishing bedding bass is the philosophy of over-finessing the fish or switching to something smaller, a drop shot or constantly changing lures. Instead of thinking about over-finessing them, think about over-aggravating them. That will spark the bite.

A lot of times, just to get that fish in the biting mood you have to fish extremely big baits—larger baits, swimbaits, big giant plastics. Let that bait do the work to get the fish aggravated so that when you put a bite-sized bait like a crawfish or worm in front of the fish they'll pounce on it.

You want to hop that big bait in front of the fish's face and get them excited—they don't have to bite it. I'll put that bait on the bed, let it sit there, shake the rodtip and get it to move around, just get their attention. I just want a reaction—maybe the fish chases the bait for a foot as you reel it out of the bed, or turns toward it when it's on the bed.

When you get a reaction, you want to reel that big bait out of there real quick and then grab the rod with the small bait and get it right in front of them, maybe hop it in their face to get them to bite it. You only have that split second of opportunity to get that fish to bite. Sometimes it takes a half hour of preparation to get that fish excited in order to get that half second where the fish is aggravated enough to bite.

You need to watch the fish closely and determine whether or not that fish is in a biting mood, and then capitalize on it. If all else fails and you determine the fish isn't going to bite, then you need to make the decision to pick up and move to another bed.

Dave Wolak is a professional bass tournament fisherman, the 2005 Bassmaster Rookie of the Year, with wins in the B.A.S.S. and FLW series. A resident of Wake Forest, N.C., Wolak travels the country as a tournament pro and lectures on targeting and catching bass. For more information on Dave Wolak, visit his website www.davewolak.com.

Bluewater anglers can utilize a species-typical behavior to their benefit. Sailfish, for instance, will "surf" the waves downsea when conditions are right. Knowing this, you would want to have spinning rods rigged with live pitch baits ready any time there is the right combination of wind and current at the depths where the sails will be hunting for food.

A fish that follows a bait for a long distance without eating it usually senses something wrong with that lure or bait, and although the fish can't quite figure out what is wrong, it's not willing to make the commitment to bite. It's your job to convince that fish that it should eat.

Let's go back to cobia. Cobia are known for "nosing" a fly or lure—pushing the bait with its nose to find out if it is real. What the fish is looking for is a reaction from the bait, and more specifically, for the bait to flee. If you're using a lethargic bait, switching out to a super lively bait will usually get you the strike. But that's not so easy to do with lures or flies.

It's a thrill to cast to aggressively feeding fish. Here, a lit-up striped marlin off Cabo San Lucas attacks a bait ball at the surface.

If the cobia touches the lure or fly with its nose, it will realize that is has been chasing an imitation bait, and then subsequent casts won't even get a reaction from the fish. But if on the initial cast you let the cobia get near to the lure or fly with its nose, and then pull it away from the fish, the cobia will pursue the offering even more aggressively, with stronger intent.

You don't want to pull the bait out of the fish's strike zone or field of vision. Just pull it a foot or two forward, but keep it in the fish's line of vision. The fish will move up just a bit faster and try to nose or "bump" the bait again. You should wait until the cobia is just a couple of inches away and then pull the lure or fly away again. Do this several times, and the cobia will get so mad it will literally charge the bait and eat it.

JSUROVIEC ©

Illustration of a cobia close to engulfing an eel-imitation Hogy lure with a weighted head for casting distance.

Determining Direction of Movement

Any time you're trying to sight cast to fish, you want to determine the direction of their movement or the direction the fish will move to feed. Some fish, pelagics in particular, will cover a lot of water to chase down their food, while others won't go three or four feet. You need to know that information before you make a cast at the fish.

Spotted seatrout commonly lunge at and grasp their prey, usually traveling no more than a few feet to catch it. A spotted seatrout sitting stationary will feed in the direction it is facing. That means it is waiting for food to approach from a specific direction. Your lure, bait or fly needs to pass within one or two feet and directly in front of that fish.

The most commonly encountered stationary feeding fish are facing into a current and waiting for their food to be washed into their strike zone. That doesn't mean the fish is going to eat the bait as it approaches. Snook sitting under the lights of a bridge or dock at night will utilize the light to locate shrimp or fish, but will regularly wait until the bait has passed before spinning around and eating it. Usually that bite takes place a few feet downcurrent of where the snook is positioned under the light.

A moving fish can be easy to target because you know the path it is going to follow. Lead the fish by casting ahead and into its path and then wait for the fish to approach the bait. With a lure or fly, you can rest that offering until the fish moves close enough so that the bait is in its field of vision and then start the retrieve. That action gives the fish the impression that it swam up on a bait which

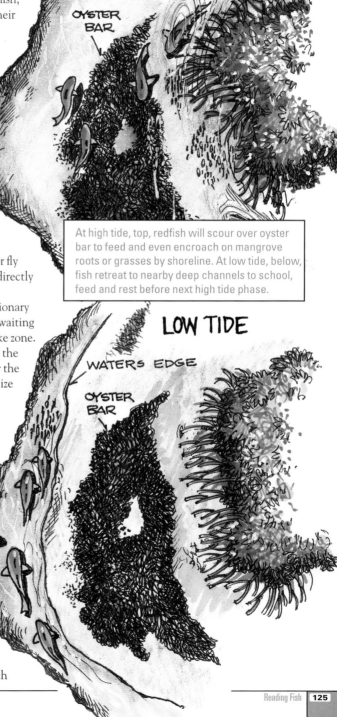

At high tide, top, redfish will scour over oyster bar to feed and even encroach on mangrove roots or grasses by shoreline. At low tide, below, fish retreat to nearby deep channels to school, feed and rest before next high tide phase.

tried to escape, drawing a reaction bite.

Not all fish move in a set direction. Schooling fish are usually the most consistent in their movements. Fish feeding along a shoreline, seawall or other physical barrier will also give you a consistent movement. In open water, fish can move in any direction and are unpredictable.

Dolphin (mahi) may swim like a bouncing pinball, changing directions as they hunt from one clump of weeds to the next. That irregular swimming movement makes them difficult to sight cast to. The downfall to the dolphin is its overly aggressive nature, so all you really have to do is get that bait into the fish's field of vision, and you will likely get the reaction you want—a take.

You'll also encounter circumstances where fish are moving up and down in the water column, whether the fish are schooled in a feeding spree

Fish feeding along a shoreline, seawall or other barrier will also give you consistent movement.

Anglers approach a seawall where currents sweep baits and predators like snook, seatrout and tarpon trap them to feed.

(striped bass or bluefish) or just moving up and down (cobia wanting to stay with a stingray). If you can still see the fish when they are down deep, you can use lures or baits that target them when they are down, but if the fish are coming to the surface to feed, then take advantage and sight cast to them when they are on the surface.

Denied, Not Defeated

If you're going to be a fisherman, you better get used to being denied by fish. There are many reasons why a fish will turn down your bait, lure or fly, but if you can figure it out, then you can adjust to the situation or improve it and possibly get the strike.

Tarpon anglers are used to getting denied. An angler may stake out his boat on a flat and cast his fly at a hundred or more fish in a day and never get a reaction, much less a bite. It's frustrating, but not necessarily hopeless. Changing the fly, the leader, direction of the cast and the angler profile are just some of the actions that could bring about a strike.

Changing your offering is one way to compensate for fish that deny a lure or bait. I've seen tarpon on the beach that repeatedly denied a purple Bunny fly and then just jumped on the first cast with a Lemon Drop. Something about the shape and color of the pattern was turning the fish off (in this case, the color, I think), and when the angler changed from a dark fly to a bright fly, the fish went on the feed.

I've seen fish deny live baits at times, even their favorite baits or the baits they're currently feeding on. In those instances the fish were seeing the heavy bite leader, and changing out to a lighter fluorocarbon leader immediately got a reaction. Freshwater trout will rise to eat natural offerings, and then deny a similar offering simply because the leader or line is too heavy or

visible. Talk to any tournament bass fisherman and they'll tell you that sight casting bass in shallow water in a clear lake required dropping down to much lighter tackle—perhaps 10-pound fluorocarbon line whereas the angler would normally fish that lake with 20-pound line or heavier. Just remember that the clearer the water, the better look the fish gets at every part of your tackle.

Fish will also deny lures or baits because they are alerted to your presence. Tarpon schooling along the beaches will move at a steady pace, occasionally rolling, milling or swimming along just below the surface. When that school is alerted to the presence of danger it will start moving faster,

A sardine, or its imitation in a streamer fly, may be denied by fish feeding on sardines if the line is visible.

rolling more and moving up and down in the water column. Eventually, if the fish feel threatened they will start slapping their tails on the surface as they roll, an indicator to the rest of the school that danger is close by and that they shouldn't feed.

Throw a live crab in front of the fast moving fish, and you'll likely get denied. Repeatedly. But back off from those fish while staying ahead of them and they'll eventually calm down and return to their normal movements. Cast a crab ahead of them, let them leisurely swim up to it and it will usually get crushed.

If a fish denies your offering but you can't figure out why, keep casting at it. The worst that can happen is the fish will spook and move off. Once in a while, the fish will suddenly strike.

Getting Fish to Lunch the Bait

You timed it right and found fish in a feeding mood, willing to crush, eat or "lunch" your offering. But there are also times when fish are lethargic, so-so or just not overly enthused to eat the bait, and it's up to you to fire up the passion in that fish to eat.

Tripletail swimming along the surface or holding in current behind a buoy are not overly aggressive for the most part. They're shy and spooky and need to be approached cautiously. Even when you approach them well and make a good cast, the fish will regularly follow a live shrimp or shrimp fly for some time before deciding to eat. You'll usually know when the tripletail is going to bite because it will turn sideways as it attacks its food.

A tripletail following or dogging a bait is probably trying to discern if it is real or natural before it eats it. If you have a live shrimp, you can help that fish make a better determination by pinching the tail off the bait, thus adding scent into the water. When the tripletail goes to follow the bait and swims into the scent trail, it'll know that shrimp is real and attack it.

Sometimes it only takes a little change in the retrieve to get a fish fired up. We've talked about cobia nosing baits and pulling that bait away from it so it can't catch or touch it, but there are times when it pays to let the bait sit in front of the fish, or just wiggle the rodtip to give it some motion. Then when the fish changes posture or moves toward the bait you pull it away.

You can use that same change-up with natural baits and lures. Utilizing a teaser plug when fishing on the nearshore or offshore waters will

Tripletail are commonly found hanging near the surface—at crab trap buoys and other structure—but they also hit baits like jigs, top, subsurface and along the bottom.

greatly increase the bites. Teaser plugs are hook-less lures that throw a lot of splash and flash into the water, but because they don't have hooks, the fish can grab them several times and not get a meal. Eventually the fish get so mad at the plug they want to kill it. That's when you toss a live bait or lure with a hook in front of the fish.

Teaser plugs are effective at keeping fish close to the boat and exciting them into a feeding frenzy. You don't just use a hooked lure the first time because you may want to be selective on which fish you're trying to catch. I have clients that are looking to catch a jack crevalle over 25 pounds in order to earn a badge in their fishing clubs. When we approach a school of 1,000 jumbo jacks in the 20- to 30-pound class milling on the surface, I can have the angler cast and catch fish until he gets the one he needs, or we can use a teaser plug to select the fish we think he needs so he only has to catch one or two.

We cast the teaser plug to the school, pull a few fish away that are all fired up to eat the teaser, and as they get close to the boat, the angler gets a good look at the size of the fish. If any of the fish are big enough, he casts his lure or bait to it. If not, we stop the teaser plug, let the fish grab it and let it go, then swim back to the school. We haven't spooked the school, so we can cast at it again and draw fish away until we can cast at and hook the fish we want.

Sometimes it's the little things that get fish to react and eat. A trout feeding on insects emerging from a stream may not eat a dry fly drifted through its strike zone because the flying insects are landing on the water downstream. All the trout sees are emerging flies, so a parachute or emerger pattern of the same fly looks more like what it is eating. The second fly drifted by that fish will get engulfed.

Pay close attention to the fish and its reactions to your offerings. That attention to detail sets exceptional anglers apart from good anglers. If you spend much time with fishing guides you'll notice that they pay close attention to the little details that most people don't even think about. But these guys know from experience that there's a reason fish react positively and negatively to baits, and they want to do whatever it takes to evoke that positive response from fish at every opportunity. SB

Hookless teaser, above, throws water to mimic an escaping baitfish which will lure out fish like jack crevalle, below, from a school so anglers can cast to select fish.

CHAPTER 10

Reading the Water

T he best sight casting anglers I know are not necessarily the best casters. True, they can usually make a good presentation to fish, but more important than being a super accurate or distance caster is their ability to read the water and act on the knowledge they gain from observation.

The water—and its terrain—will show you where to look for fish, give you an idea of what presentation you should make and even tell you where the fish are likely to feed. The ability to understand the water (more commonly referred to as "reading" the water) develops over time, but like the ability to spot fish, it soon becomes a second nature to the sight casting angler.

By reading the water, you're able to pick out the obvious spots where fish hold—a distinct advantage when sight fishing.

Fly angler casts to a fish spotted at the edge of a deeper trench on a flat— a shot produced by a good read of the water.

Reading the Depth

As he moves, a wader checks with his casts each and every sandy pothole where a trout, left, might be positioned.

Knowing the depth of the waters will tell you a lot about the area you plan to fish. Such knowledge exposes classic catch spots.

You probably have a good understanding of the fish you like to pursue and the habits or characteristics of that species. As you get a good understanding of what you are looking at when you view the water, you'll improve your ability to find fish.

Knowing the depth of the waters will tell you a lot about the area you plan to fish. Such knowledge exposes classic holding, feeding and travel areas, as well as eliminates areas less likely to hold fish. For instance, light colored sand tapering off into darker colored sand tends to indicate a dropoff—a place snook, bass, stripers and just about any gamefish can use as an ambush point.

One of the big keys to reading depth is color. Any time you're running a boat on the saltwater flats, the light brown color of seagrass is an indicator of shallow water. The lighter the hue, the more shallow the water, to the point that a light tan color is only a few inches deep. That's im-

portant to know for several reasons. One might be for navigation, and another to eliminate water that's too shallow for a big fish.

Say that you're wading an extensive grassflat and looking for areas that are deeper, where a snook, seatrout or redfish might be waiting to ambush a shrimp, mullet or other baitfish swimming through on the moving tide. If the average depth of that flat on a mid-outgoing tide is only a foot, and you're wading in water up to your knees, you're really looking for that waist deep water that will hold a trophy gamefish. The foot-deep water will be one color, brown, while the deeper holes you want to cast to are either a darker brown or almost black. Knowing that, you can wade the shallow stuff and look for fish in the darker water.

That same grassflat will likely have sandy potholes—large patches of sand that gamefish like to sit in or hunt the edges of. Those potholes will be a lighter/whiter color, and the light background will really contrast against the dark back of a gamefish making it easier for you to spot fish over the sand.

In some areas you fish, there will be long stretches of sand that allow an angler to work down the edges while remaining over the dark seagrass while looking out at the sand for gamefish patrolling the edges of the grass. You'll see that same scenario in

To navigate and to fish the numerous backcountry flats of the Florida Keys, it's crucial to have good water reading skills.

Learn to read the water depth, and you learn a lot more about what you're looking at as you move along hoping to sight cast to fish.

fresh water where bass work their way over sandy bottom and are easy to pick up as their dark green backs contrast to the lighter sand.

Color changes will also indicate different cuts or paths in the sand or grass you're fishing. On a low tide where the water gets extremely shallow, the darker holding stations, cuts and sloughs will become more obvious. These changes of depth are where you'll likely find the larger fish during the heat of the day or low tide phases. Being able to pick out the obvious spots where fish will hold give you a distinct advantage when sight fishing.

When stream or lake fishing, having the ability to read depth makes it a lot easier to locate fish and their feeding stations. The visual clues are usually water color, which often relates to bottom content. For instance, a river or stream with lots of large pebbles and boulders will have a lot of light and dark colorations to the bottom. Usually, the lighter the color to the bottom, the shallower.

Knowing that, you can look for the dark colored boulders or large rocks beneath the surface where fish are likely to hold out of the current. Then ma-

Water Clarity

Depth is not the only thing water color and clarity will tell you. Both of these visual clues can give you insight into current, temperature and the overall health of the water.

Bluewater anglers know the game. The ocean is a vast area of water, and gamefish only inhabit

Casting from deeper water, left, to shallow, a jerkbait rigged weedless works for shoreline-hugging redfish.

neuver to the best vantage point to watch those areas closely for a big trout you want to catch.

Lakes have the same characteristics as many saltwater flats, with deep holes, cuts, sandbars and dropoffs. They also have a lot of floating and emergent vegetation. Again, the lighter colors of these items below the water are usually indicative of shallow water, while the darker is usually a sign of more depth.

Learn to read the water depth, and you learn a lot more about what you're looking at as you move along hoping to sight cast fish. You'll eventually get a better idea of where the fish will sit, the colorations of fish in those areas and how to approach them using depth as your ally.

a small quantity of that water. Good anglers are attuned to visual aides that reveal where fish hold or give an indication of how those fish may be reacting to conditions and nearby stimulus.

Offshore color changes generally reflect areas of contrast. One side of the color change is healthier, has a different temperature, more plankton or diatoms—a more nutrient-rich environment for fish. Dolphin, wahoo and sailfish love to hunt color changes, and they regularly stay to one side or the other of the color change.

When you're running offshore and looking at miles of open water with little variance, a color change is a huge indicator that something is different, something that gamefish may like. So when you find these color changes you often want to fish along them while watching for gamefish.

Where estuarine waters contribute to the mix, color changes in the ocean generally go from brown or green to blue, following a lighter to darker or more vibrant pattern. The overall color of the water may be an indicator of the depth or nutrient richness of an area as well. For instance, the electric blue hue you see in the ocean is usually an indication of super clear, deep water with lots of current—and a relative shortage of nutrients. Out here, fish gather on "oases" of life, such

Just by looking at the water you can tell it's cold on the bottom, and that's a good clue that the cobia and other gamefish will likely be swimming on the surface. When presented with this scenario, anglers can wait for the sun to be high in the sky so they can see well across the water and into it, and then run along while watching for cobia swimming on top.

There's another green hue that saltwater anglers refer to as "kingfish green." It is a darker green but with a lot of clarity on the surface so that you can see five or six feet down into the water column. Kingfish green water is another great water condition to watch for fish swimming along the surface. The bait moves higher into the water column for better visibility, and predators rise to the surface as well.

Baitfish moving around the perimeter of dirty, clouded water—a perfect ambush scenario for a predator.

Dirty water, while not great for sight fishing, can tell you things as well. Water that is stained indicates a mixing of water

as seamounts or drifting patches of sargassum.

Some fish, cobia for example, tend to be found closer to shore—quite close to shore, in fact, whereas the electric blue water tends to appear with regularity only miles offshore the U.S. Gulf and Atlantic.

Cobia are also very reactive to water temperature, and dark green water is an indication of coldwater inversions. The colder the water, the heavier it becomes, which is why the coldest water in any given water body is typically found on the bottom. There are times when water in the offshore canyons is pushed close to shore, either by deep ocean currents or wind-generated Ekman transport. When that happens the water in close tends to take on a funky green hue which is easily recognizable once you've seen it a couple of times.

usually from another source, like runoff washing into a river, lake or ocean. The dirty water comes from one direction and moves to another based on elevation, gravity or tides. In a lake, bass will often hunt the area where dirty and clean water meet, prowling the edges on the clean side as they watch for prey moving out of the dirty water.

In areas of brackish water or where salt and fresh water meet, dirty water is usually a sign of where the fresh water impacts the salt, with the dirty water typically fresh. Fresh water is less dense than salt water, so it's lighter, meaning the fresh water is usually on the surface. You'll want to look deeper into the water column to spot saltwater gamefish that are going to hold in water that's more comfortable. Freshwater gamefish will likely hold closer to the surface.

From the frigatebird activity, you can tell that some bit of unseen surface structure is attracting a swarm of life.

The Role of Current

Currents play a huge role in helping you to locate gamefish. Quite a few species like to sit out of the current and wait for their food to come to them, while others like to use the current to pursue their meals. In either instance, current is the contributing factor that provides the food.

Fish that like to sit out of the current, like freshwater trout, still utilize the flow of the water to gain access to their meals. They just don't sit in the mainstream current, instead preferring to hold in an eddy, usually behind an object like a rock, log or piling, waiting for the current to push the meal into its field of vision. As the meal comes into view, the fish can decide whether to lunge out and eat it or let it go by.

Knowing this, anglers can expect to find trout holding out of the current in the eddies created by rocks or logs that block or divert the current flow. The trick here is to watch for objects that create eddies in the stream, and then look in the eddies for the fish. Once you spot a fish holding in the eddy, you want to look upstream for the seam that flows the food to that fish. In many cases the seam will be obvious, either as a distinct increase in current flow that wraps around the structure or as direction of movement to the water. In either case, that is where you want to place your cast, so that your offering flows into its feeding area.

Another good example of fish using eddies to hold out of the current involves offshore oil or natural gas rigs or water-based light houses. These huge steel rigs with pilings stretching into the water are held in place despite a moving ocean current. Fish like cobia and barracuda hold on the downcurrent side of the structure where they can remain motionless with little effort, yet can lash out at any meal that comes within their natural predatory range. Approach any of these structures knowing where the fish are likely to be holding. When you spot the

Amberjack and other species orient themselves around structure, like this tower, depending on current flow.

Different species will position around a jetty structure depending on the strength of current.

CURRENT

Where fish hold on an incoming tide will not necessarily be the same place they hold on an outgoing. Watch them and you'll learn the zones.

fish, you can make the appropriate cast that will bring your offering into the strike zone.

Any time you're approaching a fish holding in current you want to do so from a downcurrent or 90 degree angle. These fish are feeding facing into the current and are extremely sensitive to movement in their field of vision. Approach from downcurrent and to one side, and make the cast above the fish and work it in front of or toward the gamefish.

Buoys are another common type of structure that fish will utilize to hold out of the current. Fish like tripletail often hide behind crabtrap buoys looking to feed on shrimp, crabs and small fish looking to use the buoy as a means of shelter. Again, the key here is to observe the fish and then the direction of the current and let your offering play into the tripletail's feeding zone.

Many gamefish can hold in moving current because of the relative mass of their bodies or their hydrodynamic shape. Fish like snook and

tarpon sit in the shadowlines around bridges or just hold there, facing into the current along shorelines or dropoffs. These fish are holding motionless or with minimal effort while waiting for fish and crustaceans to be swept into their feeding zones by the moving water.

There's a definitive pattern to which fish hold in the current and where they are likely to be stationed based on the food items that are being brought by currents. Typically this means tides, and where fish hold on an incoming tide will not necessarily be the same place they hold on an outgoing tide. If you can spot fish holding in the current and watch them for several minutes, you'll likely form a strong understanding of their strike zone and what they are feeding upon.

Locations where you find fish holding in the current one day will likely attract fish to that same spot on a regular basis. It's a feeding station. Fish these areas frequently under the same conditions, and you'll catch fish on a regular basis.

Visual Clues for Locating Fish

All kinds of visual clues provide insight into where the fish will be holding, feeding or looking for safety or sanctuary. Remember, comfort and food are two of the main focuses of gamefish. If the sun is high in the sky, fish will be looking for shade or deeper water to protect their eyes.

As far as shade goes, docks, bridges, buoys and floating objects such as weeds or tree limbs are all good sources of shade. Fish don't have eyelids, so they're going to frequent areas that shade them from direct sunlight whenever

structure slowly, watching for fish holding in the dark shadows.

The term "visual clues" covers a wide spectrum of options, many of which we've talked about already, like color changes which indicate depth or current movements. Sometimes it's just a natural seam in the water that suggests where fish will likely hold based on the apparent pattern of where the food is flowing. Think about the fish and their feeding habits and you'll get an indication of how food can lead you to the fish.

Permit and tarpon sitting in a channel or near a bridge will face into the current eating crabs

Trees along a shoreline provide shade in heat and root-warmth in cold weather, always attracting fish to hold near them.

possible. This shade also provides some means of hiding from unsuspecting meals that wander too close to the shade-providing object.

Trees along a shoreline are a great source of shade, and just about every member of the bass family along with other gamefish like peacock bass and oscars frequent these shady areas on a regular basis. Approach any shade-providing

that are washing by in the current. The fish hold where the crabs naturally flow past, and one of the easiest ways to determine where that would be is to look closely at the floating grass.

Seaweed is one of the crab's most common means of transport. Crabs grab onto the weeds and ride the tides from one location to another, but not all weed holds crabs. In this instance,

Offshore, there is no better lead to pelagic action than a solid sargassum weedline which is really a floating oasis of sealife. Trolling along a weedline produces bites, above, as will drifting along it and casting to sighted fish with any variety of baits. Left, crab with bait stopper on hook.

you want to locate the grass that has crabs flowing with it, and then follow that grass as it flows through these channels and cuts.

Once you locate the food and its direction of movement, you can watch it closely as it flows and locate the feeding fish. From there, a hookup is as simple as positioning yourself to the downcurrent side of the fish and then make a cast that will allow the current to sweep the offering into the fish's strike zone.

Using the clues that moving or stagnant water provide will help you locate the fish you're after and often will give you an idea what the fish are eating as well as where their strike zone is. From there, it's up to you to make a good cast that will bring that offering in front of the fish. SB

CHAPTER 11

Weather's Role

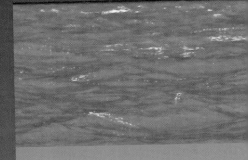

No matter what type of sight fishing you do, weather will play a key role in helping and hindering you when spotting fish. As often as the weather might change, our understanding of its processes, systems and dynamics develops with continued observation. Weather is a major piece of the puzzle anglers put together on the spot to see the big picture in order to find the fish. The more pieces you have, the easier it is to locate the fish and catch them.

Over time you'll find distinct patterns to the weather which you'll automatically incorporate into your trip's strategy. Changes in air temperature, wind or sky conditions will have an effect on your ability to spot fish.

Plan as best you can your sight fishing excursions for days when the light is going to be good.

A storm approaches, and anglers casting to a fish on a marker are about to lose their light. Time to wrap it up and run.

Sunlight and High Light

Make sure to keep the sun at your back at all times to avoid reflecting glare off the water and into your eyes.

Sunlight is a key element when looking to sight cast to fish. Sunlight penetrating into the water helps define bottom structure as well as expose the presence of fish. Without sunlight, sight casting becomes more difficult.

Plan as best you can your sight fishing excursions for days when the light is going to be good. For instance, in my home waters of Southeast Florida, afternoon thunderstorms tend to build up every single day in the summer, but their timing changes over the weeks. Best to plan trips early and expect half a day fishing.

Time of day is another key factor. When the sun is low to the horizon (either early or late in the day) the light hits the water at a sharp angle making it more difficult to see into the water with the sun at your back, and impossible to see into the water with the sun in your face as the light reflects off the water creating glare.

Make it a priority to keep the sun at your back, so that you are looking into the water in the same direction the sun is penetrating the water. Let's say you're looking to sight fish for migrating tarpon schools along the beach. If the schools normally move 100 to 150 yards from the beach, then in the morning you want to run with the sun at your back looking in, and the same thing in the evening. In the morning you'll be inshore or offshore of the fish (depending on your location in the country) and in the afternoon it will swap out and you'll be on the opposite side of the fish, either outside or inside.

During that optimum midday light the sun is penetrating the water at more of a right angle, throwing reflections off the bottom and fish in all directions. Glare is also limited during that period, as the sun is overhead and not reflecting back toward the angler at an angle.

Sunlight is not always a good thing. It can hurt

fish's eyes, so they may move away from the light, which might be to deeper water or to shade. A trout or bass, or offshore a tripletail may move its face into the shade provided by structure, not knowing that its body is still out in the bright sunlight and easy to spot. During high light, always look closely at any structure that provides shade for fish. You'll be surprised how many fish you can spot that have no idea you can see them.

Just because the best light for sight fishing is midday, doesn't mean you can't sight fish earlier or later in the day. You just have to make sure to keep the sun at your back at all times to avoid reflecting glare off the water and into your eyes. You can also switch over to high contrast sunglasses like those with yellow or red lenses that brighten the reflected and refracted light and let you see a little deeper into the water column during low light conditions.

Some of the best sight fishing takes place early and late in the day when the fish are most active. These low light conditions can be brutal to sight fish in, but they can also offer some advantages. With the sun at your back, even in low light conditions, a rolling tarpon will shine on the surface of the water. As will a cruising sailfish that sticks its dorsal fin out, or a feeding trout or striper that splashes on top. In all scenarios try to have the sun behind your back, not your face.

Low light conditions can be fine for sight fishing, but not the low light from rapidly approaching storm fronts. Fronts cause atmospheric disturbances and can shut fishing down until the turbulence passes.

How Temperature Fluctuations Affect Fish

As weather patterns move across the country they directly affect the fish, whether by raising or lowering the barometer, air or water temperatures or all of these elements.

Fish feel changes in temperature and react to those changes. A fish that is too hot or cold is going to move to an area of more comfort, and that same fish is going to be more aggressive with its feeding and movements when in the optimum temperature environment.

Barometric pressure is one of those things anglers don't think about on a regular basis, but it does have a lot of impact on gamefish. Seatrout and bluefish, for instance, like to feed heavily on a rising barometer and will do so ravenously until the barometer stabilizes. Then, as the barometer remains the same or begins to fall, the fish relax and go off the feed. Knowing this feeding pattern, you'd want to sight cast for these fish with a rising barometer. (The connection is based on observation rather than science, though air pressure can exert some influence on tides.)

Barometric pressure is just one of the conditions that triggers feeding sprees among many gamefish species. Air temperature seems to have less effect than water temperature on fish aggressiveness, although it directly impacts the water temperature over time. If the air is a specific temperature for a prolonged period—say two days or more—then it's going to impact the water temperature. After the

Proper position to the sun makes the difference in low light conditions at the day's start and sunset.

With the sun at your back, even in low light conditions, a rolling tarpon will shine on the surface of the water.

air temperature has dipped into the freezing range for two nights, the surface of a lake may begin to freeze over and the water temperature will drop. A warming trend sends water temps up, obviously, but the changes take time.

When a cold front comes through your area, you'll notice the shallow water cools more quickly while the deeper water holds its temperature longer. Conversely, shallow water also warms quicker, so when the sun is beating down on the shallows, they warm up faster than deeper water. That means fish reacting to cooler temperatures are likely to seek deeper water when it gets cold, and then quickly move to the shallows during the warm-up. Fish also seek the deeper water for relief from excessive heat, and then move to the shallows at night as the water temperature cools.

With that in mind, you can use the weather to target specific gamefish or know where to look for fish. If the air temperature has been in the 90s for a week without any rain to cool down the water, largemouth and smallmouth bass will start moving to deeper water to become more comfortable.

Something else the bass will look for is moving water, which tends to be cooler and better oxygenated than stagnant water.

Knowing this, you would want to sight fish bass in hot weather along dropoffs and in clear deep water with structure like weed beds, or in areas where there is moving water such as that around the mouth of a canal or where a stream comes in to the lake. When cold weather strikes the southern coastal states, spotted seatrout, snook and redfish go deep. If that cold weather occurs over several days, then the fish move up over shallow, dark muddy bottom to warm in the sun. In the middle of the day when the sun is high and the air still frigid, these fish are in super skinny water getting warm. As the sun goes down, they move off into deeper water that is less sensitive to daily temperature changes.

One of the biggest changes created by cold weather is a natural die-off of diatoms and other living particles in the water that can limit visibility, which is why saltwater areas seem to have clearer, cleaner water in winter. When these organisms die from the cold they sink to the bottom, increasing water clarity and thus your ability to see deep into the water column.

Air and water temperature fluctuations along with changes in barometric pressure will help you understand what the fish are doing and where their comfort zone might be, allowing you to narrow your search. That's why most exceptional anglers and fishing guides pay such close attention to weather patterns.

Wind and Other Elements

There's no doubt that the less wind, the easier it is to see deep into the water column, but unfortunately the best wind conditions regularly take place early in the day when the sun is low and depth perception deep into the water column is limited. Wind is a factor anglers fight on a regular basis when sight casting, but there are instances when wind will help you spot fish, particularly in deep water where small waves will give a relatively clean view into the water. Keep in mind that wind is only a negative if you allow it to be one. Turn the wind to your favor and you'll catch more fish.

One of the best ways to fight strong winds is to fish the lee of an area where the shoreline or other structures block the wind, allowing an angler to fish in relatively calm, optimum sight fishing conditions. The drawback to fishing the lee is that these areas may not reflect where the fish necessarily want to be at any given time. In that case, it's better to fish in the wind than fish in the desert.

If you're going to fish into the wind, it's better to fish downwind than upwind, not just because it's harder to navigate against the wind, but also because it's more difficult to make an accurate cast into the wind. That being said, if fishing downwind will put the sun in your eyes and severely limit your ability to spot fish, then you're probably better off fishing upwind because you can't make a difficult cast to a fish you can't see.

On windy days, I like to take a few minutes before I start fishing to assess the situation. That lets me gain a better understanding of the wind direction, along with the angle of the sun, and plan the best course of action. Often, I pick a spot to fish that will put both factors in my favor and give me the best opportunity to sight fish, as opposed to going where I think the fish might be and hoping to overcome the elements.

Wind on the ocean is as natural as fish in the

As air and water temperatures dip, fish adopt new patterns and anglers must adopt new techniques.

water, and certain wind conditions can actually help anglers spot fish because they're more conducive to the fish being on the surface. On the east coast of Florida, wind seems to encourage sailfish to tail or swim downsea on the surface. These conditions can be tough to fish against, but by using the wind to your favor and fishing to the south on a northerly wind, you have the wind at your back which makes for more accurate casts, and the fish moving in the same direction so you're approaching them from an angle that is out of their normal range of vision.

Just as it's harder for you to see into the water, it's more difficult for the fish to see upward through the chop. That's why many of the best permit anglers (and fly fishermen in particular) prefer the windy days over the calm days, because they can get a lot closer to the fish without putting them on their guard.

One of the key elements to this equation is to have the wind at your back or to one quarter so you don't have to cast directly into the wind, which can limit casting accuracy and distance. With the wind in your favor, you stand a better chance of making a good cast to fish that have no idea you're there. Fly fishermen, in particular, are vulnerable to contrary winds. When possible, orient the boat so that the casting arm is on the downwind side of the fly fisherman.

Speaking of using the wind for casting distance, on windy days you can keep the wind at your back and expand considerably on the lengths of your casts. That's really important when using small or very light lures or baits, light tackle or casting anything that isn't very aerodynamic that will stall in the wind. This is particularly important when fishing baitcasting gear, which will backlash easily if your offering stalls in the air in the middle of a cast while the reel spool continues to spin at the same rate.

Be aware of the wind conditions at all times, and then turn those conditions into a positive factor that improves your opportunity to sight cast. Over time, you'll understand in your home waters where different species will take shelter during different wind conditions, and how to approach them and present baits to them. You'll know at once after checking a wind and weather forecast where to expect to find fish, where not to bother even looking, and how long current conditions will persist before the next change in the weather makes it a new game again. That's the home field advantage. SB

A beautiful day on the flats, yes, but hard to fish when the fish see and feel your every move in calm, clear water.

Keep in mind that wind is only a negative if you allow it to be one. Turn the wind to your favor and you'll catch more fish.

A slight chop from moderate wind on shallow flats can allow you to get closer to fish without alerting them.

CHAPTER 12

Sight Fishing Techniques

Much of the information contained in this book refers to general sight fishing techniques, but in this chapter we look at specific styles of fishing and offer some tips on targeting fish in these areas. Things to look for, where and how to spot fish and typical scenarios are just a few of the subjects we'll discuss in this chapter.

In other words, now it's game on. The quality of the knowledge about species and conditions will only be as good as the quality of your technique and execution on the water. Some anglers say that they'd rather be lucky than good, but it's always best to first be good, and then at least occasionally be lucky.

> Now it's game on. The quality of your knowledge will only be as good as the quality of your technique and your execution on the water.

Cut down glare with a
polarizing lens to see
deep into the water to be
prepared for oncoming
fish at a distance.

Pulling a creature bait through pads, like this frog, becomes more effective when cast from a distance, below.

Freshwater Gamefish

When you're sight fishing in a lake, whether for bluegill or bass, try to make the longest cast with the lightest gear.

Any time you're fishing a lake or stream it's imperative that you move about slowly, and take your time scanning the water and looking for fish. Even relatively clear lakes have somewhat stained water that can make it more difficult for anglers to spot fish. The majority of freshwater fish are lunging/engulfing type predators, which means they move slowly or sit motionless in ambush points waiting for food to come within striking distance.

Gamefish have natural coloration that camouflages them against their surroundings, so they're harder to spot when motionless. To see them, look for movement when sight fishing trout in a stream or bass along a shoreline or over a weed bed.

Quite often as you approach these fish they will sense your presence and attempt to reposition themselves where they have a better look at you or move off slowly in another direction. By looking way ahead of your approach you can see these fish when they first start to move off and get a cast to them. Try to lead the fish and have the lure or bait move into the strike zone. The fish will usually grab the bait on the go.

Clearer water dictates the use of lighter line. In a clear freshwater lake the fish may see your standard 20-pound line. You'll know the fish are sensing something wrong when repeated good casts get denied. If that's the case, then it's time to downsize your gear.

Monofilament is extremely effective in fresh water, but in this application it pays to switch to a less detectable line like fluorocarbon, which has a lower refraction index than monofilament. You can also drop to a 10-pound braided line that has the diameter of 2-pound monofilament and is thus harder for the fish to see. In a pinch, you can use both, 10-pound braided line with a 24-inch piece of 10-pound fluorocarbon at the end. In all three instances, the odds of getting a strike improve when the fish can't see the line.

Look ahead as you approach to see feeding activity and fish moving through cover.

The same goes for trout fishing. Fish spotting the line or fly tippet is one of the major strike deterrents, particularly for larger, older fish. If you see trout rising to feed and offer the same meal but continually get turned down, it is likely the fish is seeing the leader and it's time to scale down.

One of the big turnoffs for bedding bass is movement. These big females guarding their spawning beds see well, and the closer you get to their position the less likely they are to bite. The nice thing is that bass have short memories, so if you get too close to a spawning bed and the fish moves off, you can reposition your boat a very long cast away and wait 10 minutes or so and the fish will come back to the bed. Then you can make a long cast and get the fish to eat.

When professional tournament anglers find bedding bass they rarely leave the fish. Some anglers will work a fish for an hour or more to get the bite. Ask any of them. They'll tell you the biggest thing when bed fishing is to keep the bait on the bed as long as possible—the bass thinks your lure is eating its eggs and grabs the bait to kill it, not to eat it.

Any time you're sight fishing in a lake, whether for bedding bluegill or bass holding along a weed bed, you want to make the longest cast with the lightest gear possible. Always try to approach the fish from an angle, and make slow, deliberate

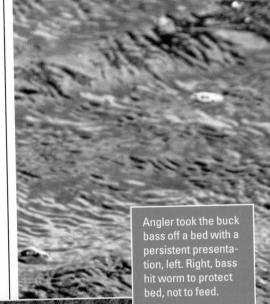

Angler took the buck bass off a bed with a persistent presentation, left. Right, bass hit worm to protect bed, not to feed.

movements. Most fish are used to seeing other animals around, but it's only when that animal gets close enough to be able to strike effectively that it poses enough of a threat for the fish to be on its guard and stop feeding.

When professional tournament anglers find bedding bass they rarely leave the fish. Some anglers will work a fish for an hour or more to get the bite.

Inshore Saltwater Gamefish

Many of the redfish

Light tackle sight fishing really began in the inshore waters of the Florida Keys where anglers would target bonefish, tarpon and permit in gin clear water. Over time, the Keys anglers

have perfected their techniques and shared them with others, who have taken them to all coastal areas and applied them to their local fishing. Now, sight fishing is common in shallow saltwater areas throughout the country. These days, many of the redfish tournaments are won by fishermen skilled at sight casting.

What the Keys sight fishing community has learned is that no two gamefish species are alike and each has characteristics that set them apart from the others. Permit, for example, like the bait thrown right on their noses, while bonefish and tarpon will bolt at any bait tossed into their field of vision. What they also found is that certain techniques remain consistent: Long casts

Angler keeps his profile low to avoid detection by wary bonefish in clear Bahamas water, below.

and deliberate body movements will improve your chances at catching fish.

Everything from seatrout to bluefish and striped bass will react at the approach of an angler, so either stay as far away as you can and still make a good cast, or approach the fish at an angle so you're less likely to be in their normal field of vision. For the spooky fish, make a long cast ahead of the fish and let them approach your offering. Even when fishing lures or flies, you can cast way ahead of a moving fish, and let it sit there until the fish moves close enough that your offering is in its strike zone. Then give it life and let the fish react to it like it just crossed paths with its next meal.

Any time you're fishing the shallows, height will help you spot fish. It's usually more productive to sight fish from a boat, because you're above the water and looking down, making it easier to see into the water column. Even the simple act of standing on your toes will at times make it easier to see fish at a distance and get a long cast off to them before they have a chance of detecting your presence.

Current can be a big key when targeting inshore gamefish, as most fish feed facing into the current. It allows them to use their sense of smell and at times inhibits the bait's ability to evade the predator. You can fish up- or downcurrent, but in either scenario you want to consider where the fish are likely to be and approach that area from the side so you don't move directly into the fish's field of vision. Stay on the fish's peripheral vision to avoid detection.

When you spot fish in the shallows, get low. Redfish, seatrout, striped bass and bonefish, just to name a few, have excellent eyesight and lowering your profile will help you avoid detection. Just don't make a sudden crouching movement. Fish see that, too.

In some locations, Louisiana for example, when fish spook it doesn't mean you just blew your opportunity to catch it. Gamefish that don't get a lot of fishing pressure are more likely to just move away from what they detect as danger and then immediately relax again and resume feeding. I've seen countless redfish in Louisiana that were spooked by the approach of a boat and the fish's movement let us spot the fish and make a cast to it, only to have it eat. In areas where the fish get a lot of fishing pressure, once you spook that fish, it's gone. Any time you have the opportunity to make a cast, take it.

The shallower the water, the more the fish will be on their guards for predators. When fish move up into the shallows they stand a better chance of detection from everything from barracuda to ospreys, so they tend to be super spooky. Sounds will draw curt reactions, as will movement. Any time you are looking to sight fish in shallow water everything you do should be a deliberate attempt to avoid spooking fish.

Redfish, top, move up into shallows on high tides to feed among the roots of grasses where crabs hide. They can be sight fished and if spooked may well return in minutes to the spot.

Beach and Nearshore Saltwater Gamefish

There are a lot of gamefish that cruise the beaches or within a mile of shore, from cobia to several shark species, as well as many of the premier inshore gamefish like striped bass and tarpon. Often the presence of these fish is part of their migratory pattern, but other times the fish are simply there because that's where the food is holding. Whatever the reason, some of the largest gamefish in the

The hookless teaser, usually in the shape of a topwater pencil popper or chugger, can be cast to the area of the turtle and then worked back to the boat with the cobia following it. As the cobia pursues the plug, the angler gets ready to make a cast at the fish. This technique requires two or more persons.

Stripers, bluefish, redfish, tarpon, sharks and mackerel are just a few of the species you'll encounter running the beach and surf zone. These

Angler in a fighting chair battles a tarpon off a beach along the species' migratory route off Florida.

Stripers, bluefish, redfish, tarpon, sharks and mackerel are just a few of the species you'll encounter running the beach and surf zone.

country are caught by anglers sight casting either from the beach or just outside the surf line.

Migrating fish like tarpon and cobia cruise selected paths that are easy to intercept. Other times a cobia might be on the back of a turtle or stingray and quick to follow its counterpart. For that reason, it's good to carry a hookless teaser plug in your boat any time you're running the beaches.

schools go on feeding sprees or "blitzes" and anglers can spot and cast to them to randomly catch fish of all sizes. Not classic sight fishing, but thrilling nonetheless.

Big schools of fish will resemble a different color than the water, often dark black or red, depending on the species. You may even see fins or the backs of fish sticking out of the water as they feed. Any

Large fish can be selected by quick casts to leaders in a school, and by using large plugs, right.

If you're fishing from a boat, one of the most valuable tools for approaching fish is a trolling motor, which allows you to get close to the fish silently while positioning the boat for the best casting angle to get a bite. Any time you approach a milling or

time you're looking at a volume of fish moving along, there are ways to pick out the fish you'd like to target or the larger fish in the school, particularly if the fish are swimming at a slow, steady pace. By watching closely, you can determine the lead fish in the school and where the largest fish are in relation to that fish, then cast to that area. Watch for the larger fins, the wide back or long stretch between the dorsal and tail fin of the larger specimens. That increases your chance of catching the biggest fish in the school and getting another shot at the school if a fish misses the first time.

Another trick you can use is to go with a lure or bait that is considerably larger than what the average fish can eat, but not too large that none of the fish would want to try. For instance, if you encounter a school of redfish on the surface that contains fish from 20 to 40 pounds, by going to a 14-inch swimming plug, you eliminate the majority of 20-pound fish that would try to eat the lure and limit the bites to the largest fish in the school. You can do the same thing with live baits.

slow-moving school of fish, you want to turn off the outboard engine and drop the trolling motor when you are several hundred yards away from the school, and then close the distance using the trolling motor. That decreases the chance the fish will detect the presence of the boat.

There are times when offshore pelagics like sailfish and barracuda move close to shore to feed, and when you encounter these fish you usually only get one or two shots before they spook. Approach these fish silently and from their periphery and make every cast count. When these gamefish move out of their normal comfort zone and in to shore they are there for one reason: to feed. Because these fish aren't in their normal feeding areas, you have to get off a cast while you can.

Offshore Gamefish

The majority of bluewater fishing is done by blindly trolling to encounter fish or by targeting a reef, wreck or other structure likely to hold fish. Then there's sight fishing, which incorporates a little of both techniques as well as live-chumming.

There are two basic philosophies to sight fishing in blue water: Either cover water or go to where you think the fish are and try to bring them to you. Both are very effective.

The cover-water game relies on cruising until you spot fish, then casting to them. That's a very effective technique for billfish as well as dolphin, tuna and sharks. Billfish are regularly encountered floating or tailing on the surface, behavior indicative of feeding in a very relaxed manner. For the majority of billfish you encounter or spot tailing, you'll want to approach from the side or at a 90-degree angle so that you can place a cast in front of the fish. If you get in front of moving or cruising fish, they'll usually go down as they come within casting range and detect the presence of the boat.

Even sharks can be spooky around boats, as the shadow of the boat casts looks like a larger predator. Sharks cruise the surface in a comfort zone, usually temperature related, so that they are not necessarily up on top to feed. Nevertheless, they are opportunistic feeders that will eat a well-placed bait and great sight fishing quarry.

With both species, it's best to lead the fish a good distance and let the fish move up on the bait. That's not always an option, so if you have to cast close to the fish, try to make your cast land to one side, but not directly in front of or right next to the fish. If your cast lands in its feeding range with a

One way of chumming to bring fish to you offshore is by diffusing frozen block chum in a net or meshbag.

These birds are feeding on baits pushed above the surface by predators—a good indicator of a potential bite.

splash, the fish may think it spooked a baitfish, and will turn to investigate, see your offering and eat.

Dolphin and tuna are fast moving pelagics, so you don't really get a lot of opportunity to stalk the fish or slowly move into position. Be ready to cast to busting or moving fish the second you see them, so it's best to have the rods rigged and an angler positioned and ready to cast on short notice.

When using live baits, you can place a hooked bait in the livewell with the lid open or place the hooked baits in one or two 5-gallon buckets filled with water and in the corner of the cockpit. Then the rods can be set next to the baits and ready for an angler to pick them up and cast to a fish.

One of the easiest ways to locate tuna is to find the birds. Feeding tuna leave pieces of fish in the water as they eat, and sea birds swoop down to pick up those morsels that are left behind. The birds can follow the tuna from high in the sky, then swoop down to look for pieces of fish when the tuna come to the surface to feed.

Anglers will use their radar or binoculars to locate flocks of birds that are traveling with the tuna and then motor over to intercept the school. Once within casting range of busting fish, the anglers can grab a rod, pitch a bait and hang on.

Birds also play a role in finding

Common practice offshore has angler, lower left, spotting with binoculars to find birds diving to feed which leads anglers to pelagic action, whether dolphin, above, or tuna, sailfish or marlin. Structure can also be spotted.

Simple spinning outfit setup to cast live baits to pelagics chummed or free roaming offshore.

dolphin. Big, free-roaming dolphin chase baitfish like flyingfish and ballyhoo out the water allowing frigatebirds to swoop down from the skies and grab the fish while in the air. The frigates follow the swimming dolphin closely, so anglers can use the frigatebirds to locate the dolphin, then cast in front of the moving fish. Since several species that dolphin feed on jump out of the water, like flyingfish, you can cast very close to a dolphin which will think one of these fish has landed in its feeding zone and get the bite.

The other sight-casting strategy offshore entails going to a structure where bait or fish congregate and starting your own feeding frenzy. This is best accomplished by bringing along some chum, either live or dead, then placing that chum into the water to attract the fish close to the boat where they can be sight cast to with your choice of bait, fly or lure. You're creating your own feeding station.

Live chum in the form of juvenile baitfish like sardines, pilchards, minnows and bunker works particularly well for everything from sailfish to snapper and grouper. Amberjacks that are holding over a wreck will immediately come to the surface to eat the chum, as will cobia. Once the fish you're targeting are on top, you can pick the fish you want to catch and either throw a live bait directly in its path or use a lure or fly of similar size and shape to make the same cast.

Any time you approach a reef, wreck or other structure you believe might hold fish you'll want to have a rod ready to make a cast. Fish are curious, and when a boat isn't around they're more relaxed and exhibiting their normal behavior, which might be to hunt on

the surface. If you're ready to make a cast when those fish first appear, you stand a good chance of catching one or more of those fish.

In the next section, we'll see how some of these same principles apply to fishing in streams and rivers. There are lurkers like pike and muskie that hold out of the current along shorelines or weeds and also prowl those areas. Then there are the moving fish like carp that are constantly on the prowl for something to eat. And lastly, there are fish like trout and bass that keep feeding stations in eddies and out of the main current where their food comes to them.

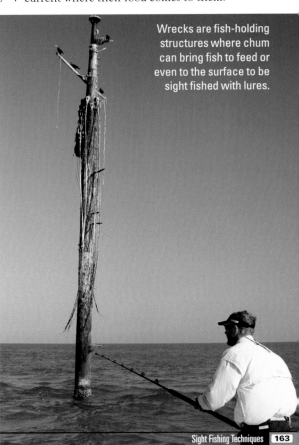

Wrecks are fish-holding structures where chum can bring fish to feed or even to the surface to be sight fished with lures.

Stream and River Gamefish

As with any type of sight casting, approach the fish from an angle, not straight on or directly from behind. It's also best if the fish are farther away or on the other side of a stream as opposed to being close by or on your side.

Fish like pike, pickerel and muskies spend a lot of time motionless, waiting for their prey to move within striking distance before they lash out and grab it. These are fish that you can make a cast past and retrieve your offering across their plane of vision. For fish that are holding motionless along a shoreline, you can cast beyond the fish but close to the bank, giving the impression that your lure or bait came from that shoreline and is now trying to work its way across the stream.

In large, slow-moving pools you may get a big member of the pike family working from one side to the other as it patrols the area for food that is swept downstream with the current. These bodies of water typically have an area of fast moving water that is turbulent, which makes for a great spot to cast your offering that will allow it to go undetected when it initially hits the water, thus avoiding spooking fish. You can also cast upstream to the next pool and work your offering back into the pool the fish is patrolling.

Scouting out rivers and lakes for bass beds, dropoffs and submerged vegetation any time you're on the water can lead to better sight fishing opportunities other days.

It's important that you make your offering look real. Members of the pike family are known for dogging a lure or fly right up to the boat before striking or turning away. A lot of anglers will make big figure eights boatside in an effort to continue having the lure moving until the fish completely denies or tries to eat it.

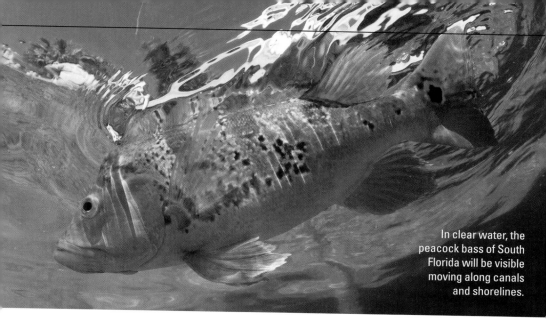

In clear water, the peacock bass of South Florida will be visible moving along canals and shorelines.

Another method is to irritate the fish by pulling the bait out of the strike zone every time the fish gets close enough for a good look. After the bait darts away a few times the fish will get mad and just charge it. Fury can be strong motivation.

Moving predators in streams or canals like carp, peacock bass and rock bass will patrol a shoreline looking for an easy meal. If they spot it, they aggressively attack. Knowing that, you want to work the shorelines. Move slowly and use any vegetation or structure to help hide your presence as you search for fish. Usually, fish are seen when they move, so take your time, scan the water repeatedly and watch for dark objects that don't remain in the same place.

When you do spot one of these fish, the most important thing to understand is the direction of movement. These fish will generally move in a well-designed direction as the fish patrols from one end of its domain to the next looking for its next meal. Once you understand which direction the fish is moving, it's a lot easier to place a cast well in front of that fish but in its definitive line of movement. As the fish approaches and the offering enters its visual feeding zone, the angler should make it come to life by imparting action on the bait, and then let the natural instincts of the fish do the rest.

Some fish, like peacock bass, may attack a lure or fly aggressively and miss completely. Once you've fired up those feeding instincts, you want to take advantage of them by casting right back into the same spot. More often than not, the fish will attack and catch the lure the second time.

Sight fishing in current is more difficult than it seems, especially if you have to reel or work the bait across the flow. Along with moving across the stream, the current will sweep the offering downstream, so there's definite eye-hand coordination that needs to take place. The best part of this is that with some practice you can speed up or slow down the offering and let the current sweep it into the fish's strike zone.

> **If you've fired up those feeding instincts, take advantage of them by casting back to the same spot. More often than not, the fish will bite.**

When trout or other gamefish set up feeding stations in swift currents there is little time for the fish to make the decision whether to strike or pass on any given food item. In this presentation, it's important that your line doesn't cross the fish's body or move across its main track of vision. Instead of having it drift over the fish's head, you want it to one side where the fish won't get as good of a look at the bait, yet still must make an eat or pass decision. SB

CHAPTER 13

Getting Tall

For sight fishermen not fishing from shore, having the right boat is a key component to a successful day. While you can sight fish from just about any boat, there are boats that are set up better than others.

Think of your boat as a tool that helps you locate and catch fish. There are lots of different tools out there, and having the right one for the job can make your fishing pursuits more efficient. A key feature of a boat built for sight fishing is elevation, which helps change your angle of view, making it easier to see into the water and spot fish.

A key feature of a boat built for sight fishing is elevation, which helps change your angle of view, making it easier to see into the water and spot fish.

From the tower of a sportfisher, there's not much the scouting angler can't see within a good range.

Inshore Boats

Guide poles from the platform while angler casts. "Bonefish at 12 o'clock!" the guide may be saying.

The classic saltwater flats skiff is a good example of a purpose-built vessel for sight fishing. The hull bottom is mostly flat, in order to draw as little water as possible. An aluminum platform installed on the transom elevates one fisherman above the outboard engine; he can use a long pushpole to propel the skiff across water inches deep.

The design has proven so effective, it's gone largely unchanged in a half-century.

Anglers began prowling the shallow grassflats of South Florida in ever greater numbers following World War II. This sunny period in U.S. history saw great advances in outboard engines, fiberglass boat construction, fishing tackle and, perhaps most importantly, personal leisure time. Also, returning servicemen brought to their new coastal homes an instinct for competitiveness; fooling an especially wary or powerful fish became, for some of these anglers, a more satisfying challenge than "meat fishing."

Fishermen hoping to present baits or flies to exotic bonefish and tarpon in the Florida Keys found an imperfect solution in post-War waves of fiberglass trailer boats. At first, anglers stood inside the boat, often on the bow, but below the gunwales. A handful of fishing guides working at the time began playing with the idea of raising the front deck and they did that by building a higher casting deck out of plywood. The raised-bow casting deck added another foot or two of height for the angler and allowed them to better see fish approaching and off in the distance.

As inshore fishing boats improved, the raised-bow casting deck became a standard of the industry. This was formalized in the late 1960s

A raised casting platform gives the angler on the bow a valuable increase in range and angle of vision on the water.

with the launch of the "Bonefisher" series by Bob Hewes Boats in Miami, Florida. Soon, many inshore boats designed for fishermen had a raised casting deck as a standard feature. There are still many boat manufacturers (like some of the aluminum boat and small boat companies) that do not include a bow casting deck on their original design, but anglers can improve on the sight fishing abilities of these boats by simply adding their own bow casting deck made out of plywood. A sturdy cooler also works.

Probably the greatest invention for inshore anglers was the poling platform, which raised the height of the person on the back of the boat and allowed them to see fish long before they approached the boat. The poling platform was also designed to allow the person in the stern to maneuver the boat silently and position the angler in the front of the boat for the best casting angle at approaching fish.

The drawback to the poling platform was that the person on the stern had to direct the angler on the bow to the fish. Often the angler on the bow couldn't see the fish until it was fairly close to the boat, which also allowed the fish to see the angler and the person on the poling platform and react to any sudden movements from either.

To counter this situation, the person poling the boat is able to use a clock face to direct the angler to the whereabouts of the fish. With the bow at the 12 o'clock position, the man on the platform states which direction and distance the fish is from the boat, allowing the angler to sight it easier. An example of what the person on the platform might say is, "Bonefish, one o'clock, 70 feet, moving right to left." That tells the angler the fish is slightly to the right of the bow, about 70 feet from the boat and moving from right to left.

As anglers poling the boat realized the value of being higher up, so did the anglers on the bow of the boat. Originally many started utilizing the cooler in the boat, placing it on the bow and standing on it to get a better vantage point and angle when looking into the water. Eventually, casting platforms were designed, and now there's a variety of bow casting platforms on the market to accessorize your boat. In a pinch, a cooler is still

better than standing lower on the bow.

Some bow casting platforms even come with railings, which allow an angler to maintain their balance when the boat is bouncing around, but the majority of casting platforms are flat, raised decks 14 to 24 inches above the deck. Two feet doesn't sound like a lot, but when it improves the visual angle it really makes a big difference when spotting fish.

This casting cage, quite high off the deck, offers stability during fish fights.

With the advent of the bay boat—with more of a vee bottom to handle rougher conditions of large bays and waterways—came the addition of the console towers. Tower boats have aluminum structures built above the console and anchored to the deck at either side of the console that allow the person running the boat to operate it from 4 to 10 feet above the deck. This considerable rise in height allows the person operating the boat to see well ahead and deeply into the water surrounding the craft.

Most tower boats have their own controls and electronics in the tower to give the operator the same advantages they would have if driving from behind a normal console, but with the distinct advantage of extra height. Whether fishing in

A console tower boat at Boca Grande Pass with angler fighting tarpon.

shallow water or deep, the addition of height really improves the opportunity to spot fish. The drawback to a high tower is that it also allows fish to see the boat from a greater distance, so the operator must make slow, deliberate movements when in the vicinity of fish, and the angler should make the longest cast possible to avoid the fish detecting the raised tower of the boat.

Pushpoles will help smaller boats move along quietly where the fish are, but for the majority of boats over 18 feet in length, the electric trolling motor is the option of choice. It's not until you use a trolling motor that you really realize its value and once you do, you can never do without it again. If you're four feet

> Skiff with a wide and clean bow gives plenty of unobstructed room for the angler to position for the cast.

short on your cast, instead of waiting for the fish to move closer and hoping it will not see you, you can use the motor to silently maneuver the boat in for a better cast. When fish are approaching the boat at a bad angle or head on, you can turn the boat or move it for a better casting angle. You can use a trolling motor for a variety of advantages, from approaching close to fish silently, to positioning the boat for a better cast, to holding the boat in place in wind or current for multiple shots at fish. Trolling motors offer a distinct advantage to sight casting anglers, and they should be a standard part of any inshore fishing boat.

The modern freshwater bass boat is similar in many ways to the flats skiff, with one noteworthy exception: With little need for a poling platform, the aft deck is left open to accommodate a second caster. A bow-mount electric trolling motor is the preferred mode of silent operation when casting over timber, weed beds and other structure. There are times, however, when sight fishing is called for. Some bass anglers find a short pushpole handy for sneaking up on bedding bass during the spawning season. The pole may be deployed from the bow or stern.

Nearshore Boats

Nearshore boats includes flats and bay boats and others suitable for fishing bays, sounds, big lakes and coastal waters within a few miles of the beach. Here, anglers often sight fish for species like striped bass, cobia, tarpon, redfish and jack crevalle. These species run big, travel in singles, pairs and big schools, and have their times when they like to travel on or near the surface.

strictly for sight fishing. But there are some things anglers can do to help them spot and approach fish when nearshore fishing.

One of the best habits to get into is running with the sun at your back, which eliminates the low angle glare off the water while also highlighting reflections like the back or fins of gamefish that might stick out of the water. Tarpon, big jacks, permit and cobia will all fin out, bob, float

Tower boats help to spot fish, but fish can see the higher profile.

The average nearshore angler fishes from a typical 18- to 24-foot boat. Many are set up with bow or stern mounted trolling motor systems and/or towers which provide a distinct advantage when sight fishing. I've even seen anglers create their own temporary tower out of a wooden ladder to improve their vantage point.

Not all nearshore boats are set up with sight fishing in mind. In fact, the majority of anglers sight fish on occasion or use their boats for a variety of fishing and thus don't have them set up

With the advent of the bay boat—with more of a vee bottom to handle rougher conditions—came the addition of the console towers.

or roll. Keeping the sun behind you at all times will help you catch sight of these fish.

It's also best to do your sight fishing when the sun is high in the sky and the angle of the glare off the water is eliminated, while colors and reflections are highlighted. A school of stripers or redfish is almost impossible to see and easy to run past in low light conditions, but by midmorning, the schools stand out as dark or coppery masses in the green of the water.

Some fish also push water, like cobia and

redfish, which will swim just below the surface. These bulky fish "push" or "hump" the water, exposing their presence. These pushes are easier to see with the sun at your back and on the glass calm days or early mornings when the wind is down, which does add merit to an early start to the day.

A real step up: a custom built spotting tower that is affixed to the deck.

In open water conditions, a pair of stern- or trim-tab mounted trolling motors provides some advantages over the single bow-mount: more power, ability to place the boat between the fish and the motor (thus blocking any sound) and pivoting more easily into the wind. Fly fishermen have more room at the bow for their flyline, too. The drawback to these systems takes place in moving water like inlets where keeping the boat facing into the current is easier when pulling the boat as opposed to pushing it, especially when there is a side wind to contend with.

Nearshore gamefish traveling on the surface usually follow a straight path, which makes it easier to position the boat ahead of the fish and wait for them to approach. It's always better to have the fish swim up to you as opposed to approaching the fish. It's less threatening to the fish which makes them more likely to eat. You can also use the trolling motor to position the boat to one side of an approaching fish or school of fish, so that you stay out of their direct line of vision while setting up for the optimum casting angle.

Some of the most commonly encountered fish you'll run into while nearshore fishing include

cobia, which are often swimming slowly on the surface; tarpon, which migrate along the beaches in everything from single fish to random schools; permit, which are usually encountered as singles, pairs or large schools; jumbo jack crevalle, which are found in large schools swimming on the surface; redfish, found swimming on top or pushing the surface; striped bass, which are fast-moving, blitzing gamefish; and bluefish, which also blitz ravenously, but can be seen as large dark clouds of fish or walls of big fish swimming on top. That's just to name a few. All of these fish can be sight cast on a regular basis by spotting the fish and then approaching them quietly at a good casting angle.

Offshore Boats

Under ideal conditions, any boat can fish offshore, from a small skiff to a massive sportfisher. If the ocean is calm enough, it's fishable in just about any seaworthy vessel. That doesn't mean the best boat for sight fishing is any boat you can get offshore in. By far, the boats set up with towers, large open bows and open cockpits are the most effective for sight fishing. Just look at the South Florida livebait sailfish tournaments and you'll get an idea at how effective these boats are at catching fish, many of which come by spotting them first, then casting a live bait to individual or groups of fish. All the top tournament boats for live-baiting sailfish have towers and keep someone up top to spot fish at all times.

Whenever there's a northerly wind off Florida's Southeast coast in sailfish season, sailfish will come up to the surface and "surf" downsea. When these fish are on top they're easy to see from a tower, and the captain or person in the tower can direct the anglers to cast a live bait into the path of the moving fish. The tower not only gives a better vantage when looking down, but also out across the horizon, as the extra height places the person in the tower well above any swells or waves so they can look deep into the water column. The days when boats catch 10 to 20 fish, better than half of them are usually taken by sight casting.

Along the Pacific Coast of California and Mexico, boats targeting striped marlin, blue marlin, swordfish, tuna and sharks, utilize towers

The tower gives a better vantage when looking down and also across the horizon, as the height places the person above swells or waves.

Here, the captain in the tower can look down on the action behind his boat and alert anglers to approaching fish and strikes as they happen.

to spot fish swimming just below the surface of the waves or big schools of fish blasting the water out to the horizon. The higher you get, the better view you have deep into the water as well as off towards the horizon.

The same goes for sight casting big sharks or tuna in the offshore canyons along the East Coast. From high in the tower anglers can spot tuna flashing or "shining" below the surface, or busting the surface a long ways from the boat. Height also helps in spotting flocks of birds off in the distance, as it changes the angle and makes darker colored water the background.

In all these instances, sight fishing equates to spotting or locating fish and then pitching baits or lures into their path in hopes of getting a strike. As important as it is to see and locate fish, it's even more important to be able to make a good cast at them, and that requires room to move about and cast. Open decks or bow spaces, as you'll find on larger center console boats and sportfishers, allow the angler to move to the front of the boat to get the best casting angle and distance as the boat approaches the fish. If

All the top tournament boats for live-baiting sailfish have towers and keep someone up top to spot fish at all times.

Ready with rods at the tower console, the angler not only gets a good view, but also gets the first shot to cast to fish.

Sailfish anglers are on the lookout for sailfish tailing down the face of waves, ready to present live baits to them.

the boat is moving parallel to the fish, the cockpit can be one of the best locations for anglers to cast from, and don't overlook the advantage of making a cast from the tower, where the fish can be plainly seen.

The key benefit to all these sight fishing boats is to improve the position of the angler looking into the water and the casting angles when attempting to catch fish. Just a few inches of elevation can really improve your ability to see farther into the water column and spot fish swimming along on top or just below the surface.

Once you spot the fish, it's up to the captain to approach the fish without spooking it and then position the boat so that the angler can make the longest, most accurate cast possible. Long casts and good angles will get you more bites! SB

CHAPTER 14

Sight Fishing On Foot

Just because you aren't fishing from a boat doesn't mean you can't be an effective sight fisherman. Sight fishing may offer advantages to those who can get higher to spot fish, but it also favors those who can move around easily and change their angle of approach. Quite often, the best sight fishing opportunities come to those who are wading or fishing from land.

Whether you're fishing from beaches, bridges, banks, roadsides or wading off shorelines into rivers, lagoons or lakes, you know that there a lot of opportunities for fishing on foot that boaters simply miss.

For every inshore and beach gamefish there are times of the year when the fish are more available to anglers looking to sight fish from shore.

Toe to fin with a big redfish, top, and right, releasing a permit. Fishing on foot gives you the water-level view.

Beach Fishing

Any large fish holding close to shore will be alert to unnatural movement.

For every inshore and beach gamefish there are certain times of the year when the fish are more available to anglers looking to sight fish from shore. In Florida waters, snook and tarpon for example, are encountered along the beaches during the summer months when the ocean and Gulf are calm and the fish are spawning and migrating to and from those spawning areas. In the summer, anglers can walk to the inlets or passes, fish the beaches or the spillways and encounter fish "laid up" or cruising in relatively shallow water close to shore.

Snook are often in the trough right up against the beach, and can be seen laying in ambush or slowly cruising for food. Beach or shoreline anglers can walk slowly and deliberately and see the fish, then maneuver for a good casting angle and pitch baits ahead of the fish and work them into the strike zone.

Tarpon are more often encountered rolling or cruising just outside the first bar, although there are times in late summer when the fish will feed on glass minnows within a few feet of dry land. Slow, deliberate movements are again the key, and as an angler spots a fish laid up, rolling or slowly moving, they can put a cast in front of the fish and move the offering or let the fish swim up to it. In both these scenarios

Knowing the travel lanes and troughs at a beach in advance will help you spot fish working at dawn.

In southern salt water, species will hold and feed at different strata off the beach.

Mullet and other larger, migrating baitfish attract the attention of tarpon and snook.

Snook often feed right in the wash and in the first trough off the beaches in their range. Anglers approach stealthily.

the strikes are extremely visual and explosive, as are the reactions of the fish after the hookset.

Any large fish holding close to shore will be alert to unnatural movement, so most anglers position themselves away from the water. On most sloping beaches and shorelines that usually means strolling higher up and looking down into the water, which is a better vantage point for spotting fish. Because you're not close to the water, the fish are more accepting of your presence, but they are still very attuned to movements.

There will be times when fish approach close to the angler without being seen, until they are very close and the angler finally sees the fish and knows that he is in the animal's visual range. That leaves the option of making a soft cast using just the wrists to avoid movement, or letting the fish pass and then making the cast. The latter option is usually the best, as the angler will be out of the fish's main field of vision, and thus the fish will likely be

Red drum forage for blue crab on outer bar.

Snook, jacks in shallow water beneath anchovy school.

Pompano scouring the wash for sand fleas.

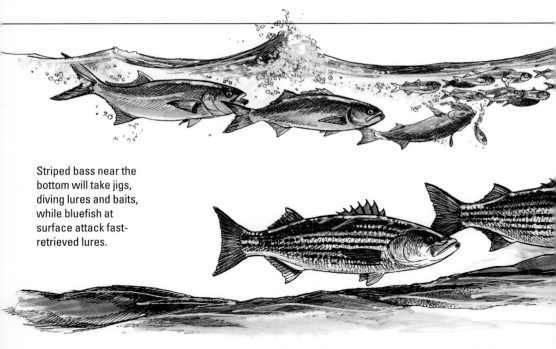

Striped bass near the bottom will take jigs, diving lures and baits, while bluefish at surface attack fast-retrieved lures.

more relaxed and willing to strike. That being said, I've seen some huge fish caught by anglers who simply flipped a bait a few feet and in front of the fish, and had it immediately blasted.

Similar opportunities take place along coastal shorelines of the Gulf and Atlantic for redfish and striped bass, with both species cruising the surf line or holding in position in the trough. Position of the fish and its relative movements will offer some keys to getting a bite. Consider, for example, where the fish is in the water column.

If the fish are on the bottom, jigs or diving lures that swim deep and can create little puffs of sand when worked across the bottom will often help these fish spot the bait. Fish closer to the surface might be more aggressive and react better to surface lures or subsurface lures that can be paused in the strike zone. The direction a fish is facing or moving tells the angler where to place the cast so that the offering moves naturally into the fish's feeding zone.

Any time you're beach fishing, if you're coming across fish that are cruising the trough or shoreline, it's better to position yourself at a good vantage point for spotting fish and then remain in the area. Let the

Big snook caught right in the trough in the summer in Hobe Sound, Florida.

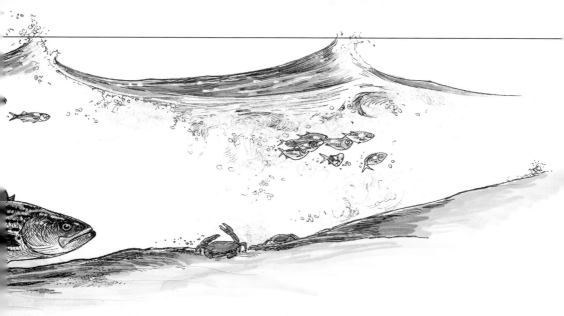

fish come to you, which allows you to spot them at a distance. Look for dark or slightly different coloration in the water that is moving, and be ready to cast before the fish comes close enough to see you. Conversely, if the fish are laid up or holding in position to strike out at their prey, then walking along and covering water will give you the most shots.

The more beach fishing you do, the better you'll get at making those decisions and concentrating on spotting fish. You'll develop a comfort zone of where you like to position yourself from the water, and will naturally move to it. In the middle of the day, when the sun is high and you can see deep into the water column, it may pay off to step into the water a few feet and move parallel to shore as you scan for fish. As the situations dictate, your movements and reactions will soon become as natural as those of a successful hunter moving silently in a forest.

If you're already in a good position to cast at a bonefish that swims into view, you'll be less likely to spook the fish.

Wading Grassflats and Docks

Wade fishing presents some great sight fishing opportunities across the country. For many anglers, the classic scenario is stepping into an ice-cold mountain stream in search of colorful freshwater trout. But it doesn't stop there. You can wade coastal flats and lakes just about anywhere there's hard bottom and have good sight fishing.

In the Northeast, striped bass come into the bays and hunt the sandbars and flats on a regular basis, allowing anglers great opportunities to see, cast to and watch the fish eat their baits. In the South, snook, seatrout, redfish, pompano and a host of other gamefish are available on the grass-flats for anglers wading and watching for sight-casting opportunities.

One of the drawbacks to wade fishing is that you

Wading Tools

No doubt the appeal of wading stems from its low cost and simplicity. All you need is one outfit and a couple of lures or baits and you're ready. But there are a few tools that can make your wading more comfortable and more productive. Your dress will depend on the temperature of the waters and the depths where you wade, but the basic gear includes a good extendable leash net, a floating fish bag or a stringer to keep your fish if desired, and some means of keeping your tackle, leader material and pliers either above water or dry in a watertight box in your clothing or waders.

Also popular are wading belts to carry an extra rod or two and either a good pair of wading booties or waders. Small dry bags to hold cell phones and keys are also handy.

Top, the warm-water wader wears a belt to hold additional rods rigged with alternate baits. Middle, the belt up close and left, two styles of floating fish tools.

As the situations dictate, your movements and reactions will soon become as natural as those of a successful hunter moving silently.

This wade fisherman offers a lower, considerably smaller profile and less noise than boat anglers.

These cold-water waders are keeping the sun at their backs and using neoprene waders to preserve energy and extend trip time.

are standing in the water as opposed to above the water, so your angle of view into the water is diminished. You can improve your sight casting opportunities when wading by waiting until the sun is higher in the sky, but that may not be the best time to target fish that aren't active in the heat of the day.

If you're wading at first light or in low light conditions, it's better to look for visual clues to cast to than for the actual fish itself. Pushes of water made by big fish moving around in the shallows, fins popping out of the water, scampering baitfish or diving birds are a couple of the clues that will alert anglers to the presence of fish. Other times, it's better to put the sight fishing on hold as you cast to sandy potholes in the grass, the edges of rockpiles or reefs or other obvious gamefish ambush points.

As the sun rises and light penetrates the water, wade fishermen will get a better view into the water column and can spot fish lying in ambush or feeding. As with all sight fishing, slow, deliberate movements are imperative to prevent being spotted by fish. Move along carefully and silently, scan-

ning the water as far out as you can see for the fish in that zone. The farther you can spot the fish from yourself, the better the opportunity to catch it.

Wade fishing does offer the advantage of a considerably lower profile than fishing from a boat or shore, so the angler is harder for fish to see and they will often swim up close to the angler and still eat. Any time you spot a fish nearby that you think you can get a cast to without your casting movement spooking the fish, make the cast! With effort comes the reward of some of the most exciting strikes you'll ever see.

Any time you're wade fishing, structure will be your friend. Structures like rockpiles, reefs and docks provide sanctuary to baitfish and a hunting area for gamefish. In addition, docks provide shade from the sun and a shadow area that helps fish hide. Gamefish regularly patrol or hunt structures, so you should too!

When approaching structure, try to have the sun at your back so you have a better chance of spotting fish. Approach the structure slowly, scanning the area around and inside for fish, while trying to position yourself for the best cast to that area. You control the casting angles, so approach the structure from an angle that gives you the best cast to any fish that might be around.

For docks, it's a good idea to approach at an angle where you can make a cast down the dock or at specific sections, and then proceed to look for fish in those areas one at a time, repositioning for a good cast at the next section of dock as you move along. Docks that have boats will usually have deeper water where the boats are located, and those are spots where big fish like to sit. Also look at the shady areas, scanning not just for fish that might be nearby, but fish that might be holding in the shade with a part of their body extending into the light. You'll see redfish and big seatrout with their tails extending out of the shade, which gives you an idea which way the fish are facing and where you should place the cast.

Fish will also hold tight to the pilings and use them for cover and an ambush point. Everything from flounder to redfish instinctively position close to

In the subtropics and tropics clear-water flats and white sands present visually stunning bonefish settings for waders.

structure where it's convenient to lunge out at prey as it nears. Above all, move slowly and look the area over well before moving on. Fish sitting motionless are a lot harder to spot than fish that are moving, so take your time. Watch for shadows and dark objects in the water that look like branches or logs or have more than one color. If you see something that has the possibility of being a fish, make the cast—you have nothing to lose.

ProTip - Sight Fishing the Flats

Ironically, the four most spoken words from an angler on the bow while sight fishing are, "I don't see it." That's because the most common error made while searching for fish in shallow water is to try to look at fish, not for fish.

The real key to successfully spotting fish is to learn to trust your eyes to pick out a subtle difference while constantly scanning side to side and in front of the boat. Then when a possible radar blip is detected, you tighten up the scope of your focal point. Veteran guides and anglers can identify a species and determine whether to pursue it or dismiss it in a millisecond.

A much-overlooked contributor to better in-water vision is repetitive fishing of the same shallows. When you learn the details of a flat, you subconsciously see movement or shape to more carefully scrutinize. The more you fish a flat, the more you become familiar with its habits so that in any given tides and conditions you already expect to find certain animals doing specific things in the "red zones" of each area. Effectively spotting fish starts with the ability to see things clearly before they happen, based on past experiences.

Always begin your search by scanning long distances in front of you for obvious interruptions of the surface water. If you spot anything that looks like it might be fish pushing, focus on exactly what is causing that nervous or funny water.

Tailing fish are the easiest to spot and classify, while less obvious ripples can be tougher to work with. Small, tight wavelets are usually baitfish, while a hump of disruption, especially with several points of origin and direction, is likely your target species.

Muds can also be a bit more complicated. A big thick swath of dirtiness is usually a ray, but check it out carefully, depending on where you are fishing, as redfish, bonefish or permit could be in tow and waiting to pound a smaller critter stirred up or scared up by the ravenous dig. Smaller, thinner and more quickly dissipating smokiness could mean bonefish or permit.

Even if you have not locked onto the outlines of fish due to low light levels or a bad angle, you can still connect the dots and plot a course ahead of the puffs—almost always upcurrent—and then cast to and hook a good fish that you really never saw.

It's the attention to small details when sight fishing the flats that gives certain anglers and guides their enviable "eagle" vision that we all would like to have. Look for the changes, learn the topography and little nuances of the flat and watch for signs of fish, and you'll be a lot better at sight fishing gamefish on the flats.

Captain Mark Krowka is a perennial tournament-winning flats guide based out of Islamorada, Florida.

Bridge Fishing

Bridges are some of the best places to sight fish from shore. They provide the structure fish like to use for cover and areas that hold baitfish and other food items. In addition, bridges funnel current and are the avenues to open water, so crustaceans like shrimp and crabs that are drifting with the current or attached to weeds

The best part of this style of fishing is that it's very visual. You see the fish when they're holding and feeding. You can position yourself to make a cast that will bring your offering right into the strike zone. Then you watch the fish attack it.

Tarpon, snook, seatrout and striped bass like to hold in the darkness along the shadowline and then use the tide to bring their feeding opportunities within striking range. Knowing that, you should position yourself in an area where you can watch the shadowlines closely for feeding fish. These fish generally stay in the same area, so when you see a fish move into the light to grab a bait or reposition itself, you should be confident that fish remains in the same area. That will allow you to cast upcurrent and allow your offering to flow downcurrent to the fish in a natural manner. As it traverses the lit area, you want to maneuver the lure or bait so that it will enter the shadowline

This young bridge fisherman lights his scene with a headlamp as he unhooks a small snook at night.

The majority of great sight fishing around bridges takes place at night, when gamefish wait to ambush.

are regularly swept through these areas. Most importantly, at night, bridges have lights which shine into the water and create shadowlines which gamefish can utilize as camouflage while watching in the lights for their next meal. A fish can sit on the dark side of the shadowline facing into the light and see prey from a distance, move within the shadows to intercept the prey, and then strike as the prey enters the disorienting darker area. It's a definite hunting advantage for gamefish.

The majority of great sight fishing around bridges takes place at night, when the gamefish are holding high in the water column to ambush fish and crustaceans moving through on the surface.

where you last spotted the gamefish feeding. The strike will come as the bait enters the shadow.

You'll also want to pay strict attention to how the food items are flowing through the light and into the dark areas and any consistent lines of travel that will create feeding lanes for the fish. If shrimp are flowing through the light on the surface, ensure your own baits are drifting freely in the same manner. Use light enough fishing line that the baits can naturally swim on the surface.

You'll see baitfish come through the light on a regular basis. Watch how those baits flow through the light and the areas they frequent. For instance, finger mullet come out of the darkness and when

Pay strict attention to how the food items are flowing through the light and into the dark areas.

Anglers, perched under a bridge at night, present baits along the shadowlines.

Tarpon and other gamefish hold just downcurrent of the shadowline near bridge pilings.

they hit the lighted areas they sometimes will stop swimming and drift through the lighted area with the current. If that's the case, and you're throwing a topwater lure that looks like a mullet, you'd want to make your cast into the darkness, work the bait until it hits the light and then pause the lure, letting the current move it into the shadowline. That's the natural action of the bait, so that's the retrieve that will look the most natural and get the strikes.

At most bridges, the fish like the upcurrent side, but that's not always the case. Some fish, like seatrout, seem to like the downcurrent side better. In tropical waters, permit, too, like to sit behind the bridge pilings out of the current and eat as the food moves by. And some bridges have open areas that divide the lanes and allow light to shine down in the middle of the bridge, and fish will use these areas. So every bridge is different, and you want to spend a little time checking every shadow and light opportunity presented.

There will also be some sight-fishing opportunities that take place around bridges during daylight hours. Ambush feeders like permit and tarpon will sit behind or around pilings, while "grazers" like sheepshead and pompano can be seen feeding on the shrimp and crabs attached to the pilings. More often than not, the fish will be in the shaded areas of the bridge where the shadow blocks the midday sun and makes it more comfortable for the fish to be feeding close to the surface. As with any type of bridge fishing, you want to observe the feeding patterns of the fish, then replicate them with your cast and bait presentation.

Pier Fishing

Piers offer some great sight fishing opportunities: cobia swimming past the pier; barracuda, snook, pompano and snapper using the pier's pilings as ambush or feeding points. Pier fishing offers the distinct advantage of height, which means anglers have a great angle for looking into the water. If the water is clean and clear, as it is around a lot of ocean and gulf piers, that makes the fish easier to spot.

Anyone who has fished from a pier in the Florida Panhandle during the spring knows the cobia game. Cobia cruising in a westerly direction outside the surf line regularly come within casting distance of the structure, allowing anglers a chance to sight cast the fish as they swim by. Bright 1- to 3-ounce jigs are the lures of choice, with anglers casting in front of the fish or beyond them and working the lure into the fish's line of sight. Good polarized sunglasses help anglers spot the fish, which initially appear as dark or light brown shadows moving just below the surface. The first angler to spot the fish will shout out, and is offered the first cast at it.

The pilings and lights from piers regularly attract baitfish, and gamefish come close to feed on those baits. It's not uncommon to see king and Spanish mackerel, bonito and even the occasional sailfish circling a baitfish school adjacent to the structure. When you see those fish working the bait pods, you'll want to get a bait into the middle of the school, then work it to the outside edges of the bait and even into the open water

Nets Are Essential

Few experienced bridge anglers fish without a landing net, likely because at one time in their careers they lost a great fish due to the lack of a good net. Nets that lower to the water's surface serve another important purpose in addition to the primary one. Nets—along with careful handling— also help to keep in good shape fish that are over- or undersized and meant for release. This snook measured 30 inches, legal during Florida's open season.

where it will stand out and be an easy target. Fish like snook and snapper utilize the pier's pilings as protection from predators as well as ambush points for food, and will regularly hold tight to the pilings directly below the pier but in the vision of anglers looking down. When you see these fish near the pilings they are usually facing the direction they are watching for baitfish, so your cast should be out ahead of the fish and in its direct line of sight, with the lure or bait working its way back to the pier right in front of the fish.

Pompano and sheepshead are known for hunting pilings for small shrimp and crabs. Pier anglers can see not only where the fish are holding but also how aggressively they are feeding. Then it's a simple act of dropping a lure or bait right into the fish's strike zone and waiting for the bite.

Like bridges that cast a light onto the water at night, many fishing piers have lights on them to attract baitfish, shrimp, crabs, squid and other forage items. Any time you have large concentrations of food in one location, you can expect to have gamefish in the area taking advantage of that food source. Night-time action around piers draws a lot of gamefish, including tarpon. Under the lights the fish cannot detect your presence as easily, so

Old bridges, above, and other long-standing waterside structures, below, are great fish attractors.

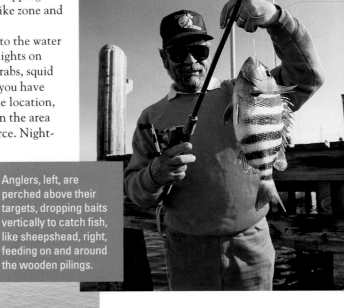

Anglers, left, are perched above their targets, dropping baits vertically to catch fish, like sheepshead, right, feeding on and around the wooden pilings.

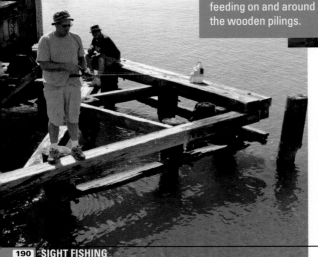

they can be more aggressive and easier to hook. Pier tarpon usually position themselves in the lighted areas on the outside of the baitfish schools, waiting for a good opportunity to rush the school and feed. At times, you can spot individual fish holding motionless in position and then make a cast that will bring your lure or bait right into that tarpon's strike zone.

Weakfish and spotted seatrout are two species that are regularly attracted to piers at

night, as they move in to feed on small baitfish and crustaceans that are also attracted to the lights. Both species of the drum family can exceed 10 pounds, and when the big ones come in they tend to move slowly in and out of the lights, selecting their forage before lunging after it. That allows anglers to pick individual fish to work baits in front.

In the Gulf states you'll also find a lot of small fishing piers and lighted docks on inshore waters. These piers attract redfish and seatrout in big numbers, but aren't especially good for sight casting to individual fish. You can, however, see the trout and reds moving in and out of the lights, and can cast to fish in a general area with a good chance of hooking up.

Inshore piers are typically in areas exposed to tidal changes, so you get moving tides that funnel the food into the lights. The fish like to sit on the upcurrent side of the lights, often using the structure as an ambush point, striking out at shrimp and baitfish as they move into the lights. Any time you're fishing from a pier or dock, you'll want to move about gingerly to avoid sending a lot of vibrations into the water that will alert fish to your presence. As always, make the longest cast possible, which also limits the opportunity for fish to detect your movements. Make the cast upcurrent of the fish, and work the offering into the light and into the fish's strike zone.

There's one last thing I want to mention about pier fishing, or any fishing done under artificial lights. Manmade light shines in different light spectrums than sunlight, so fishing lines with fluorescent properties tend to stand out in this type of lighting. Monofilaments and fluorocarbons are not as effective because of the direct and reflective light, so in most instances you will have to size down your leaders and bite tippets to get the bite. If you're fishing under the lights and have fish move toward your lure or bait then turn away at the last minute, they are likely seeing the line and you should downsize or switch to a clear leader material.

Fishing from foot is one of the most productive means of sight casting gamefish, and very rewarding for anglers. There are plenty of options where you spot the fish, make the cast and literally watch the fish eat the offering, then watch it react as it feels the sting of the hook. And in the world of fishing, it just doesn't get better than that. SB

> **Fishing from foot is one of the most productive means of sight casting gamefish, and very rewarding for anglers.**

CHAPTER 15

Putting It All Together

S ight fishing is a visual and exciting way to target gamefish, and it's practiced all over the world. It's not only effective, but seeing the fish and watching it react to your offering is one of the most rewarding and memorable ways to catch a fish with hook and line.

   Let's look at some of the top sight fishing gamefish from around the world—the pinnacle of the sport—and where, when and how to target them and a few of the top locations for these fish.

Seeing the fish and watching it react to your offering is one of the most rewarding and memorable ways to catch a fish with hook and line.

Top, a redfish tails in shallows by a roseate spoonbill. Right, bonefish feed in water not much deeper than their bodies.

Tarpon

The silver king can be found from Central and South America across the Gulf of Mexico to Florida, the Caribbean Islands and also in Africa. Along the Eastern Seaboard, they range as far as Virginia, with the best action from Florida to North Carolina.

Florida is one of the best U.S. states to target tarpon, as the warm tropical climate of South Florida is home to resident fish of all sizes. In May, the fish migrate through the Florida Keys, pushing their way up either side of the state through June. Of all the top sight fishing locations, the Florida Keys probably offers the most consistent tarpon action for anglers fishing lures, bait or fly.

These fish push through the flats and channels of the Keys in small schools or strings of fish that are easily spotted as they move within casting distance in anywhere from three to six feet of water. There's also great sight fishing for tarpon along both sides of the Florida peninsula as the schools migrate along the beaches in clear water that's anywhere from 8 to 15 feet in depth. For the biggest sight fishing adventure, try Homosassa in May for the giants, with fish exceeding 200 pounds traveling through the area that month.

Tarpon can be sight fished along beaches of both Florida coasts, as well as in passes and near bridge structure. The world's most famous tarpon spot may be Boca Grande Pass in Southwest Florida.

Florida is one of the best U.S. states to target tarpon as the warm tropical climate of South Florida is home to resident fish of all sizes.

In jade green waters, you'll first see a school of migrating tarpon like dark dashes over white sand bottom.

Sure Signs

Tarpon are much tougher to hook and to catch than they are to find. Their well-known behavior of rolling on the water's surface, right, is not a feeding act but a way for them to gulp air to oxygenate, often during migrations or elevated water temperatures. Flashing tarpon by bait, below, shows feeding.

Permit

With clear water and good supplies of fish, there are times and places where anglers can cast at more than 100 permit in a day.

The southernmost waters of Florida and much of the Caribbean and Central America are home to pristine flats that attract permit in large numbers. With clear water and good supplies of fish, there are times and places where anglers can cast at more than 100 fish in a day. But for the most part, any time you see permit, whether alone or in a school, is a good

Anglers targeting permit in these areas usually fish from a skiff, poling the shallows while silently watching for feeding fish. Whether throwing a live crab or a crab fly, it takes a good presentation and lots of luck to sight fish permit in the shallows.

One of the best places to target permit is on the flats off Key West and the nearby Marquesas in late winter and early spring, when the big fish push up into the shallows to feed. Windy conditions allow anglers to approach within casting distance to fish that are tailing and finning on the surface. Line up your cast and take a shot.

day. Considered one of the most difficult fish to catch on any tackle, permit are the holy grail of fly fishing, with fish regularly denying the fly.

In spring and early summer, permit are frequently encountered offshore around wrecks and reefs in large spawning aggregations, but the most exciting and challenging sight fishing occurs on the flats in less than three feet of water. Two of the best permit fishing locations are the Florida Keys and Belize, where fish search the shallows for crabs.

Big permit, left, gather in spawning groups over wrecks and reefs in their range and can be sight fished when schools surface.

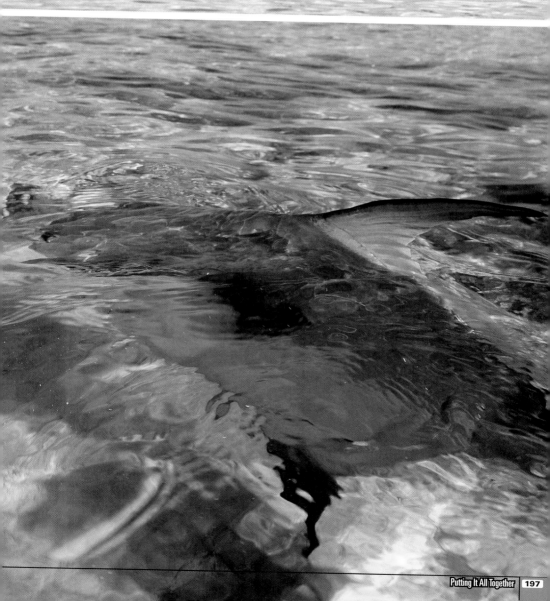

Sure Signs

The permit's sickle-shaped tail is high and sharp. The V-shaped dark tail is also highly visible just beneath clear water. The permit's green-gold upper body blends with its habitat, but flashes silver when moving. In channels, at times permit "moon," or float.

Redfish

Red drum, a.k.a. redfish, roam the coastal estuaries from Texas to North Carolina, with the larger breeder fish moving out into the Gulf of Mexico or open Atlantic when they reach a weight of 12 to 14 pounds. The bays and inshore waters of Texas and Louisiana have immense redfish populations, with fish available for sight casting year-round.

In fall, the Carolinas host huge schools of giant spawners that come in close to shore to feed.

In fall, the Carolinas (North Carolina and the Outer Banks area in particular) are host to huge schools of giant spawners that come in close to shore to feed. Similar schooling behavior of big fish takes place on both coasts of Florida in November and December.

Of all the great sight fishing opportunities for redfish, the marshes of Louisiana offer the right combination of numbers, clean water and willing fish. Sight casting 30 to 50 redfish in a day is not uncommon from October through February for anglers using lures, live bait or fly.

Charleston, South Carolina also offers large numbers of fish in a tidal marsh setting, with clear water and lots of fish in the winter months. For consistent sight casting opportunities at big fish, it's hard to beat the waters of the Mosquito Lagoon in East Central Florida, where unique schools of landlocked spawning redfish roam the flats all year.

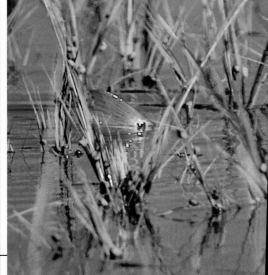

Sure Signs

Redfish feed in shallows and clear water throughout their range. The tail and body coloration—yellow-brown to blue-tinted to reddish-gold, depending on locale and season—along with distinctive black spots near tail make the fish easily identifiable.

The orange-red tails of red-fish are unmistakable when the fish are tailing to feed, singularly or in a school. The humps of water indicate a single fish's movement.

Inshore, schools can mass for spawning and feeding activity and remain in local areas for days or longer. Left, redfish tailing in marsh grass at flood tide.

Striped Bass

During the heart of winter, striped bass fishing in Virginia and off the coast of North Carolina can be fantastic.

With a range along the eastern seaboard north from the Carolinas, striped bass can be caught on a regular basis as far south as Jacksonville, Florida. The best action on stripers takes place in the Northeast, with top sight fishing opportunities along the beaches for fish of all sizes or in the bays and sounds for schoolies.

During the heart of winter, striped bass fishing in Virginia (particularly in the Chesapeake Bay) and off the coast of North Carolina can be fantastic, with lots of fish of all sizes feeding along the beaches. Some of the best sight fishing action for striped bass takes place in Long Island Sound during the fall, when the fish move into the shallows and wade fishermen can pick the fish they cast to with any type of light tackle.

You'll also find great sight casting opportunities for schooling fish off the coast of Massachusetts in summer and fall, with a large contingent of surf anglers even targeting the fish on fly. The islands of Nantucket and Martha's Vineyard are tops.

Sure Signs

Stripers are often identified by a combination of factors—their speed, size, their action of pushing wakes and crashing baits, and their positioning versus inshore structure. With bodies wide for their length and dark backs above white or silver sides, they are readily visible when in clear water.

Anglers casting t
an ambush point
for stripers along
shoreline, top. Up
left, school fish m
ing out of a chann
and lower, stripe
surface feeding c
Montauk, Long Is

Spotted Seatrout

Texas anglers in Matagorda and Galveston bays regularly sight cast seatrout over 10 pounds.

On grassflats like this one seatrout will sit motionless in a pothole or sand patch waiting to ambush baits. Contrary to lore, gator trout are early and midday feeders.

One of the most popular coastal gamefish from Texas to Virginia, the spotted seatrout is a great challenge for sight casters, particularly when targeting the larger trophy fish. Texas anglers in Matagorda and Galveston bays regularly sight cast seatrout over 10 pounds, and some of the islands in Calcasieu Lake along the Texas-Louisiana border offer similar sight casting opportunities for big fish.

For action, it's hard to beat the spotted seatrout fishing in Texas or Louisiana, particularly in the spring when the wind is blowing and the water warming. But one of the best places in the world to sight cast trophy seatrout is in the Indian River Lagoon area of Southeast Florida from Stuart to Cocoa Beach, where the big fish move into the shallows during the winter months to warm up and can be sight casted in the middle of the day using bait, lure or fly. Anglers working the shorelines with mud bottom that are facing into the sun can cross paths with as many as 60 trophy seatrout on a good day. The fish sit close to shore in water less than two feet deep, and anglers can cast from a distance and get the fish to eat.

The fish sit close to shore in water less than two feet deep, and anglers can cast from a distance and get the fish to eat.

Sure Signs

Smaller seatrout are often made visible by their topwater slashing of baits in channels, bays and along beaches in their range. At night, anglers target them by sight as the fish feed in the lights of docks and piers. Larger gator seatrout can be sight fished in the shallows in clear water as they wait, motionless, at ambush points or as they cruise slowly, with almost imperceptible movement, through grasses and over sand bottoms. Look for their shadows, movements and their silhouettes from a distance as you approach likely haunts.

Texas anglers anchored off the beach can find schools of seatrout by their bait-busting action.

Bonefish

onefish are a common flats species in tropical waters from South America through Central America, South Florida and The Bahamas. Bonefish have been caught in Africa and many of the South Pacific Islands as well.

South and Central America offers flats fishing for mainly small bonefish, while larger specimens are found in The Bahamas Islands and South Florida on a regular basis. For sight casting to large schools of bonefish, it's hard to beat The Bahamas Islands, where clear water and pristine flats are home to schools of fish that may number in the thousands. Anglers here can throw bait, lures or fly with great success. Some days, a single angler may catch 20 or more bonefish up to seven or eight pounds.

South Florida waters including Biscayne Bay and the Florida Keys are also home to outstanding sight fishing for bonefish, and in particular,

Bonefish are common in tropical waters from South America through Central America, South Florida and The Bahamas.

Anglers wade a tropical flat in search of bonefish, especially looking for the shapes of bodies and shadows over the sands, and the bonefish wakes and tails over the seagrasses.

for larger trophy fish. These fish receive a lot of fishing pressure, and sight casting them can be as challenging as it is rewarding.

While not known for huge numbers of bonefish, the islands of the South Pacific that stretch from New Zealand to Hawaii are home to decent trophy bonefish populations, with islands like Aitutaki offering compelling scenery and vast sight fishing flats. Between the scenery and the huge fish, sight casting bonefish in this region is the trip of a lifetime.

Nose down, feeding on the bottom into the current, a bonefish grubs up a meal and exposes its sharply forked tail to the air.

Sure Signs

Silver lateral scales reflect the bottom, and dark dorsal bands mimic patchy seagrass. That makes it tough to see bonefish. Experts look first for small disruptions of the surface water, such as ripples against the grain of the prevailing chop. In very shallow water, feeding bones may flip their tails above the surface. Over sand or marl bottom, bonefish moving directly toward you or away will resemble dark dashes, while fish moving across your field of vision may give off momentary flashes.

Cobia

obia can be found along the coastal United States from Texas through Virginia, with strong annual migrations of fish taking place in the Gulf of Mexico and Atlantic Ocean. Large fish are consistently encountered along the beaches of the Florida Panhandle during the spring, where boats cruising outside the surf line

The big springtime run on the Florida Panhandle is likely the best opportunity to catch a cobia of a lifetime from a boat or pier.

and anglers fishing from piers sight cast to fish that may exceed 100 pounds.

Along the Atlantic beaches from the Florida Keys to Jacksonville, cobia also make consistent annual migrations, with fish traveling south through the area in February and March, and then moving back north in May and June. They reach coastal Georgia and the Carolinas during the summer months, and a great run of fish takes place in the inshore waters of Charleston Harbor.

On occasion, cobia will travel inshore, following tides through the deep inlets and passes in areas like Charlotte Harbor and Tampa Bay on Florida's west coast, where the fish push into the shallows and are often seen swimming on the backs of stingrays on the flats. These fish can be sight cast on a regular basis, just as the migrating fish along the beaches and offshore found swimming on the surface. Look for stingrays, sharks or turtles as indicators.

Texas and Louisiana offer great cobia fishing, particularly in the spring and fall around the offshore oil rigs. Of all the great opportunities to sight cast cobia, the big springtime run on the Florida Panhandle is likely the best opportunity to catch a cobia of a lifetime from a boat or pier.

Big cobia in shallow water nearshore are a great thrill of U.S. saltwater sight fishing.

Free-swimming cobia at the surface, left, are often—understandibly—mistaken for sharks. Angler in the tower scans the water for cobia, ready to cast a jig to them.

Sure Signs

Cobia are often surprise visitors to boats nearshore and offshore, whether the anglers are chumming or not. They'll rise to the surface at the transom and often take refuge beneath the boat itself. When sight fishing for cobia along beaches or at structures, anglers learn to quickly recognize the dark brown backs of the fish in their various shades against different colored waters. When cobia are on the move, they can be mistaken for sharks. The best way not to miss them is to have a jig ready to cast.

Big manta rays often come with trailing cobia.

Jack Crevalle

Schools of jumbo jacks can be found around the oil rigs off the coasts of Texas and Louisiana.

One of the toughest inshore/nearshore gamefish in salt water is the jack crevalle, a species that ranges from South America through Central America, the Gulf states and southern Atlantic Ocean. These fish are tough fighters whose fight grows exponentially with their size, so that a 20-pound fish is considered more than twice as tough to land as a 10-pound fish using the same tackle.

Inshore sight fishing for jacks mainly takes place along seawalls and docks, with anglers casting to busting fish, as opposed to schooled up or singular moving fish. In Cape Canaveral, Florida and Charleston, South Carolina sight casting anglers can encounter large schools of migrating trophy fish in the 25- to 40-pound range finned out on the surface. These fish can be sight cast to using lures, baits or fly, with large poppers and surface plugs the top offerings.

From December through June, migrating jacks can be found along the beaches and just offshore from Key West to Sebastian Inlet, Flori-

da where they can be sight cast on calm days when the schools are finned out on the surface. Similar schools of jumbo jacks can be found around the oil rigs off the coasts of Texas and Louisiana during the summer.

For sheer sight fishing excitement, the fish off the Florida Coast in springtime are hard to beat, with schools of anywhere from 50 to 1,000 or more trophy fish swimming counterclockwise and finned out on the surface at regular intervals. Anglers can throw topwater lures for spectacular sight fishing action, or use hookless teasers and the bait-and-switch tactic to pick out singular fish on fly.

Sure Signs

While sometimes mistaken for permit when they're schooling at the surface along beaches, jack crevalle have darker bodies, brighter yellow tails and more elongated bodies than their jack-family cousins. They are also recognizable by their shorter dorsal compared to the height of their tail fin, but most of all by their raucous slashing and smashing of bait schools when they're on the attack. If the ocean looks like a washing machine because fish are feeding, it's probably a large school of big jacks on bait.

A big jack like the one above should not be underestimated in its power and stamina in a fight.

Big schools of jacks feeding voraciously literally move oceans. The water will hump up and be visible from a distance. Their yellow tails are also obvious.

King Mackerel

Annual migrations of king mackerel take place along the Gulf and south Atlantic states from Texas to North Carolina, with consistent sight fishing mostly limited to casting to schooling fish.

Annual migrations of king mackerel take place along the Gulf and south Atlantic states from Texas to North Carolina, with consistent sight fishing mostly limited to casting to schooling fish. There are occasions during the summer months when kingfish move close to shore and feed on baitfish schools in all these states. They can be encountered cruising below the surface where they can be sight cast using live bait.

Large schools of kingfish can also be live chummed using juvenile baitfish, a common practice in South Florida and the Florida Keys, in particular off Key West, where the fish can be found in tight schools over shallow reefs. These fish come to the live chum, and can be caught using live baits, lure or fly, with

Kingfish will launch out of the water in hot pursuit of baits, and anglers can start the action by chumming.

anglers casting to individual fish as they move through the chum line.

During the fall and early winter months, trophy kingfish exceeding 50 pounds migrate across the Gulf of Mexico and into the waters of Mississippi, Louisiana and Texas, where anglers fishing offshore can sight cast to busting or skyrocketing feeding fish. Similar schools of fish can

The maw of a kingfish never forgives, especially not when there are schools of baits to tear up. Anglers find kings around structure and favorable current breaks.

be encountered off the Florida Keys in January and February, and off the coasts of Georgia and the Carolinas in the summer and early fall.

While the best sight casting opportunities lie with those live chumming in areas like Key West in winter, the huge volume of trophy fish off Louisiana in late fall and early winter offer the chance to cast to, hook and fight huge fish in multiples whenever the weather permits.

Sure Signs

Anglers target kingfish by finding the structure, temperature and water conditions that the fish favor. Kingfish will sometimes be found at the surface feeding on bait schools or when they've been chummed to the surface by anglers. Their missile-shaped bodies and gunmetal gray/silver tones and pointed snouts are built for speed.

Sailfish

One of the most rewarding offshore game-fish for sight fishing anglers, Atlantic sailfish are found in the Atlantic Ocean from the coast of Africa west to the southern coastal United States and the Caribbean side of Mexico's Central and South America. Pacific sailfish, which grow larger than the Atlantic sailfish, can be caught from Central through South America.

The best sight fishing opportunities for catching sailfish come with casting at tailing fish, although trolling hookless rigged natural baits to bring fish to the surface where they can be sight cast using fly tackle is a common practice off Central America. For tailing fish, it's hard to beat the fishery along South Florida from Stuart to Islamorada, Florida Keys when the fish migrate from north to south starting in December, with the best action off Broward, Dade and Monroe counties in springtime.

Winter through early spring are the best times to target Pacific sailfish off Central America, with outstanding sight fishing opportunities in Guatemala, Costa Rica and Panama waters. Multiple shot days are the norm, and anglers catching five to 10 sailfish in a single day are common when large concentrations of fish are encoun-

tered balling baitfish.

The spring migration of Atlantic sailfish off the coast of Isla Mujeres, Mexico offers anglers fishing bait-and-switch or sight casting to sailfish balling bait. Shots at 20 or more fish in a single day are common. The best fishing takes place in the middle of the day when the sun is high and it's easy to spot fish on the surface or balling bait.

Look for a dark shape, often described by captains as a "black garbage bag." That garbage bag might hover in your spread, or the fish's dorsal or bill might surface near one of your baits.

Sure Signs

The long bill and rectangular fin of a sailfish are unmistakable, especially if a fish is feeding on the surface or whacking a teaser. A common scene, the "free-jumping" sailfish is a tipoff that you're in the right area. Sailfish holding deep are elusive, as the refractive properties of water distort the profile of the fish.

There is no mistaking the bill and dorsal of a sailfish feeding on baits below diving frigatebirds.

The best fishing takes place in the middle of the day when the sun is high and it's easy to spot fish.

Dolphin

Anglers fishing out of Costa Rica, Guatemala and Mexico regularly sight cast trophy dolphin around floating trees and baitfish pods. Big fish are extremely aggressive and powerful.

Dolphin fish, a.k.a. mahi-mahi, range across the Atlantic and Pacific, mostly in the warmer currents of the world. They are fast-growing, open water pelagics that cover lots of water.

Great action on dolphin can be had from the Carolinas south through the Florida Keys and Bahamas, as well as in the open waters of the Gulf of Mexico. On the Pacific side, Central America offers outstanding action on mahi of all sizes, with large fish very common.

In the United States, you'll find the best dolphin action in South Florida and the Florida Keys from April through June, with May the peak season for numbers. The largest fish come through in April, although big fish are regularly encountered throughout the year.

You can sight cast to dolphin around weedlines, floating debris and under diving birds, with the most consistent action taking place around weeds and debris, where the fish station themselves to feed on the small baitfish and crustaceans attracted to the floating items. School dolphin holding around the weeds can be caught using live bait, lures or flies, and larger dolphin are often caught while live chumming offshore.

Anglers fishing out of Costa Rica, Guatemala and Mexico regularly sight cast trophy dolphin around floating trees and baitfish pods. Big fish are extremely aggressive and powerful, so heavy tackle with large line capacities are the norm when chasing the larger fish.

Big bull dolphin are caught by anglers sight casting to them, often times when anglers are already casting to smaller fish. Below, a big tree found offshore can be approached and fish sighted just below the surface.

Sure Signs

There is no mistaking the technicolor blaze of a dolphin or a school of them in blue water. It's one of the most amazing sights in all offshore fishing. Most often anglers target dolphin around structure, current breaks and temperature breaks, and feeding birds point to dolphin also. Binoculars, left, will significantly increase the range of your vision offshore.

Tuna

Sight fishing for tuna takes place all over the world, with outstanding action in the United States off Louisiana, Florida, North Carolina and most of the Northeast. The wide variety of tuna species allows anglers to target everything from 10-pound fish to 100-plus-pounders, with anything larger stretching the boundaries of sight fishing tackle.

In the winter months, bluefin tuna school off North Carolina, and can be caught using lures, bait or flies. While the angler does not sight cast to particular fish, pitching at schools of tuna busting the surface and leaping from the water is extremely exciting sport.

A similar fishery for big yellowfin tuna exists off the coast of Louisiana, with anglers running 60 to 100 miles offshore to sight cast to busting fish close to offshore oil rigs. The majority of anglers use big spinning or baitcasting gear with topwater lures or poppers, and watch as the fish rise to the surface to explode on the offerings.

Off Florida, the blackfin tuna bite in the Florida Keys from winter through spring can be outstanding, with boaters live chumming fish to the back of the boat where they are fed live baits, lures and flies. Blackfin tuna exceeding 30 pounds, along with scores of little tunny can be drawn to the back of the boat. The angler times the cast to the fish they want to catch.

> **A fishery for big yellowfin exists off the coast of Louisiana, with anglers running 60 to 100 miles offshore to sight cast to busting fish close to offshore oil rigs.**

Sure Signs

Sight fish from 8 miles away? Sort of... Radar is used to find birds wheeling over a tuna frenzy. At the scene, tunas move so quickly it's next to impossible to target individual fish. Instead, cast lures toward frothy surface busts, or chum fish into close to the boat, where you'll have a chance of seeing a fish take your bait.

A yellowfin tuna caught in The Bahamas by chumming the schools close to the boat with chunks of bait. The Bahamas run takes place in the early spring through the summer.

The sunlight strikes a big yellowfin tuna as it arcs out of the water in pursuit of bait.

Black Bass

California is one of the top destinations for sight fishing bass in the country.

While you can consistently sight fish black (largemouth) bass in just about every state, Florida, California and Texas are known for their populations of trophy fish. These three states offer a plethora of sight casting possibilities, including bedding fish (January-March) and schooling fish (September-November.)

The clear, shallow lakes of Florida offer great sight fishing opportunities for fish that are easy to see as they move from one piece of vegetation to the next. Spawning females topping 10 pounds are sight cast to on a regular basis using lures, while large pre-and post-spawn fish can be caught using live shiners.

In Texas, shallow shorelines and deep, structure-filled lakes offer a variety of sight casting options from bed fishing the big females to pitching lures or flies to fish cruising along the shorelines. Many of the Northeast lakes also offer these great sight fishing conditions, although to smaller fish on average.

California with its massive reservoirs and winding delta system allows for consistent sight cast-ing to fish of all sizes as the bass move up to the shorelines, docks and other structures to feed. Big fish, big numbers of fish, and actively schooling, feeding fish on the surface all make California one of the top destinations for sight fishing bass in the country. SB

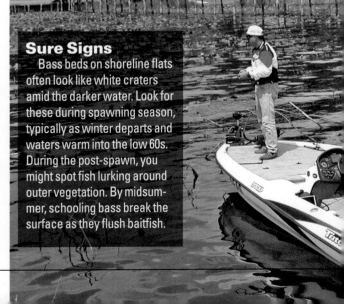

Sure Signs

Bass beds on shoreline flats often look like white craters amid the darker water. Look for these during spawning season, typically as winter departs and waters warm into the low 60s. During the post-spawn, you might spot fish lurking around outer vegetation. By midsummer, schooling bass break the surface as they flush baitfish.

ProTip - Sight Fishing Fresh Water on Fly

Sight fishing with a fly rod in fresh water is a game of pitting the instincts of a wary water creature against the reasoning, seasoning and technology of a human being. Get it right and you prevail, blow it and you fail.

There are two primary schools of sight fishing freshwater fish—fishing to active feeders such as trout keying in on an insect hatch or carp feeding on fallen mulberries, and targeting predator fish that feed on other fish, birds, mammals and amphibians. Distinct as these two approaches to catching freshwater fish on a fly are...they share some basic fundamentals to success that if heeded and practiced will travel well across species and geography and help tip the success scale into your favor.

The golden rule in this game is that a fish unaware it is being fished for is the most catchable fish. Read that again. Burn that rule into your collective angling consciousness. A fish unaware of your presence is far more likely to be fooled into eating your offering. Basically, be as stealthy as humanly possible. Most unsuccessful anglers act as bumbling idiots. Don't be one of them.

Seems really simple and it is in theory. Putting it to practice is the challenge. The five P's apply well here: Proper Preparation Prevents Poor Performance. Fly rod sight angling in fresh water is a study in being properly prepared. From experience I can tell you some days are diamonds and some days are duds. We humans can not make the fish active...we can only prepare our own selves to take advantage of whatever opportunities present themselves during our time on the water.

Understand the habits and traits of the fish you are trying to catch. This is called seasoning, and the more familiar you are as an angler with a species of fish, the more likely you are to make successful decisions when you get a good shot.

When you arrive at the water you plan to fish, stop and study the water and surroundings before you start to fish. Watch for telltale signs of feeding activity or fish holding in the current. Remember, a fish unaware it is being fished for is the most catchable fish, so a little time spent observing what is happening before entering the water will be rewarded with productive shots at willing fish.

Understanding the water you're fishing is also critical to success. Gather as much intelligence as possible about the lake, stream or river you will be on prior to your day on the water. What is the water temperature? Is the water stained or clear? Where are the likely feeding stations?

Observe other anglers and how they work the water. I always welcome the opportunity to study what other anglers are doing no matter their skill level, watching their processes and looking for successful happenings. Studying other fishermen will occasionally show you what to do, but more often what you will learn is what not to do. Both are important lessons. SB

Brad Bohen has been a freshwater fly fishing guide for the last decade, most recently specializing in hunting musky with a fly rod in Northern Wisconsin. His passion is living the fly fishing life and sharing that life with others. His business, Musky Country Outfitters (www.MuskyCountryOutfitters.com), is all about putting fishy people together on fishy water and making the most of it.

He lives with his English Setter and a band of guides known as The Musky Tribe near Hayward, WI in the spring, summer and fall and travels the country in the off-season chasing fish.

CHAPTER 16

Conservation

Sight fishing is one of the most rewarding techniques in fishing, and as you learn more about it, the little nuances of the technique become second nature. As you increasingly catch more fish, you'll have to make conscious decisions on how you handle fish and whether you keep them to eat or not.

It's too easy to get caught up in the moment and throw more dolphin, cobia or seatrout into the boat than you really need, or even want to clean. One important mark of a good angler is the ability to respect the resource while still keeping fishing challenging and successful.

Every fish we chase has an intrinsic value, one we cannot put a price on.

A redfish about to
be released, above,
and right, divers re-
searching the growth
of transplanted cor-
als on the reef.

The Future of Fishing

We need to respect the fish that bring so much to our lives. Respect them by handling them properly and by protecting them.

In just about every corner of our country the fisheries are under constant strain to keep up with habitat destruction and angler demand. It's up to every angler to be a steward of the fishery, to handle fish with care and spend the time to revive fish before release to assure those fish will survive to fight another day. By now, just about everyone knows a fish is too valuable a resource to use only once, and it's through conservation and strong fishing ethics that we are able to keep the populations of different fisheries healthy.

As you become more proficient at sight fishing, there will come a time when you have the species dialed to the point that you can catch more than most anglers are accustomed to and more than the legal limits. Despite the fact that you are bailing the fish, you need to make a concerted effort to handle every fish you catch with care. I can't tell you how many fishing guides and professional tournament anglers I've seen nonchalantly toss a fish over the side without spending the time to make sure that fish is revived and healthy. The same goes for constantly catching fish and keeping them, when you already have enough fish to eat at home.

By practicing conservation and releasing fish, we will enable our fisheries to grow, or to at least maintain the status quo.

We need to make sure we respect the fish that bring so much to our lives. Respect them by handling them properly, making sure a hook is out, the fish are revived and handled properly at all times. And most importantly, we need to educate other anglers so that conservation becomes the commonly accepted practice in a fishery. Living and fishing by example and teaching others is the direct link to improved fisheries and a more enjoyable fishing experience.

An Argument for Releasing the Big Fish

Spotted seatrout normally live about seven or eight years. A 10-pound seatrout may be seven years old, while a 5-pound seatrout may be the same age. The larger fish just grows faster for some reason, but whatever that is, we want those fast growing fish in the population so that their progeny grow.

The larger a seatrout is, the more eggs it releases, so those larger, faster growing fish can lay more eggs than the smaller fish. That means double the egg pro-

A state researcher at a dock measures a redfish caught by an angler for stock assessment studies in Florida.

One of the joys of fishing is passing down knowledge to a younger generation, knowing that they will enjoy it for years to come.

duction and double the growth rate of a 5-pound trout of the same age. So who wouldn't want those bigger fish in the population?

A similar argument can be made for fish size regulations and slot limits that may assure the largest fish survive to repopulate the species. By assuring we allow for a specified breeding population we are improving the recruitment into the fishery, so why not utilize the largest fish that produce the most eggs to do that? Smaller slot sizes allow for harvest of a fish after it has spawned one or two years, and then protects the largest fish, thus assuring great genetics and volumes of eggs make it back into the fishery to grow up themselves.

Releasing the big fish also means there's a possibility of coming back and catching that fish again when it's even larger. Whether that's by you or another angler, by setting the big fish free you enable others as well as yourself to enjoy the catch of the largest fish in the species.

During my youth I spent a lot of time chasing big snook in South Florida. I fished hard and put in a lot of time, and honed my skills to the point that I caught a lot of big snook on a regular basis, mainly because that is what I targeted the most. It fed into my ego at the time, and I was quickly known as a local hot shot for catching big snook.

One night I saw a big fish on the shadowline of a bridge and pitched a No. 619 Cisco Kidd lure upcurrent of the fish's position. The fish struck the lure with force, and in a short time I had it on the bridge next to me. This was at a time when most anglers who targeted snook ate every one they caught that was within the legal size limit and very few anglers ever released snook, much less the big ones that they could brag about.

This snook wasn't remarkably large, probably 27 or 28 pounds, and I'd certainly caught lots of larger fish, but I had to leave town the next morning so I knew I wouldn't be able to eat it. There was a big crowd of locals on the bridge standing around the fish and admiring it, when I walked it over to the side, slipped it into the water and let it go.

It was no big deal. No one said a thing. But for the next 10 years I couldn't go to that bridge without hearing someone say, "That's the guy who let that giant snook go."

In my eyes it wasn't a remarkable catch. Not what I'd classify as a giant snook, but everyone remembered it that way because the fish was set free. And everyone there was hoping to catch that fish now that it was even bigger. Those are the rewards of setting larger fish free.

The Value of a Fishery

Every fish we chase has an intrinsic value, one we cannot put a price on because of all the economics involved and the fact that it's difficult to put a price tag on the happiness, relaxation, family unity and general outdoor enjoyment that comes with being on the water fishing and catching fish. Suffice to say, without it, many of us would live elsewhere, in some community where we can enjoy the time on the water and the joys that come with it.

So what is the value of a fish? Is it the food value? The economic value it brings to the community through gas, ice, food, drink, boat, lodging and tackle sales? Is it the happiness it brings to those who spend time on the water fishing? Or is it

ProTip: Get Involved in Conservation

At some point, most of us that stay involved with recreational angling will get involved in conservation at some level. Whether it is because we want to protect a particular honey hole from being ruined, or we are attached to the idea that we want to share our love for the sport with future generations, fishermen and women are usually excellent stewards of our sport and its environment. Unfortunately, most of us do so just like we fish—independently. Consequently, the vast majority of the non-angling public views us as nothing more than "users of the resource." This is true of private citizens as well as law-making, elected officials. Perhaps eliminating this misconception is the most important reason for joining a club that is accomplishing responsible conservation.

Conservation clubs are almost as varied as the many fish we pursue. Some are gigantic organizations that work at the national level or higher; others are local clubs that have very focused goals.

Large organizations, such as the Coastal Conservation Association (CCA) or the American Sportfishing Association (ASA), play an important role in advocating for anglers at the policy level. They might also have local chapters that meet and discuss ways to support their important overall mission statements. Groups like this are critical, because they are often our only hope of putting a live body in position to counter threats to recreational fishing at state or national policy levels.

Closer to home, local conservation clubs and groups are just as important if not more. They are often formed as a reactionary response to some local project or policy that would result in disaster to regional fishing areas. These clubs are the place where you can expect to roll your sleeves up and get dirty, both figuratively and literally.

Protecting a particular beach, river, or mangrove forest might not be as sexy as shaping national policy. But it is often more personal and rewarding, and most of the individuals you will meet at this level are volunteers, working for nothing more than the hope of maintaining or improving fishing conditions for future generations.

Very often, the most active angler-friendly local conservation clubs are nothing more than your fishing club. If you have no experience with conservation at any level, this is probably the best place for you to start asking questions. If your local club doesn't have an active conservation component, they frequently allow outside conservation groups a few minutes during their member meetings, which are fantastic ways to learn about various issues. Some conservation groups like the Snook & Gamefish Foundation (SGF) work at both the policy level as well as the local level, and maintain an active schedule of seminars at fishing clubs in an attempt to engage local anglers.

Before you put your time and money into any organization, spend some time to research the organization. The mission statement is the first place you should look—a clear, concise statement that leaves no doubt as to the intent of the group should be your first requirement. Matching an organization to your greatest passion or concern is important if you want to stay involved for the long haul.

Not many people understand the interconnectedness of coastal or wetland ecosystems, and the impacts of various human interactions has on them, as recreational anglers do. Joining a conservation club is our best chance of "connecting the dots" between habitat protection and fishery management so that our angling rights are protected while ensuring a healthy fishing future.

Brett Fitzgerald
Communications Director, The Snook & Gamefish Foundation and author of Sportsman's Best: Snook

It's important to follow gamefish laws and support the fisheries.

found in the opportunity to commune with nature? I'd say it's all of the above and more.

With the advent of super markets we're no longer dependent on fishing as a means for a meal. We can just stand in line and purchase everything from meat to fish to vegetables and more. That doesn't mean we don't get enjoyment from bringing home a meal of fresh fish. However, the value of a fishery whether for pleasure or food is completely dependent on the quality of the resource. In other words, if you can't catch fish on a semi-regular basis, most people would quit fishing.

That's why it's important to follow gamefish laws and to do our best to support the fisheries. If we want to have the option of catching fish and even once in a while taking them home for dinner, we need to make sure there's a strong population of fish to target.

One of the things that makes a community great is the strength of the bonds among the people who live in that community. When the members of your community have a strong bond to the outdoors, spend time on the water, and are concerned about the habitat of the fisheries, they are usually more involved in and better stewards of the areas simply because the health of the area is directly related to what they enjoy.

Whether you keep fish to eat or release everything you catch, it's important to keep in mind that everything you do to make sure that fish survives when it's released increases the chance it will help repopulate the species. From following good hook-setting and tackle practices to handling fish with care, the more we think about the fish that just brought pleasure into our lives, the better its chance of survival. That includes offshore gamefish, like barracuda, which tend to be treated with irreverence when not edible.

I can't tell you how many times I've seen anglers gaff bonito, barracuda or big jacks because they didn't want to handle the fish or didn't have a dehooking device on board. Killing the fish means one less part of the food chain exists and one less breeder exists to keep that chain growing. Even if a fish isn't edible it has merit, and you'd be surprised at how much joy a jack crevalle or little tunny can bring to someone's life.

So as anglers we need to think of conservation first, and the enjoyment that comes with fishing second, because without the conservation we won't have the large populations of gamefish to enjoy. SB

A small fish to a small child can still mean a great deal to the future of the fishery.

Docklight snook
face upcurrent
as they feed.

SIGHT FISHING

INDEX

INDEX

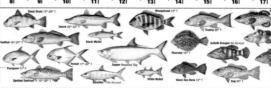

SIGHT
FISHING
DVD

The Sportsman's Best: Sight Fishing DVD brings the pages of the book to life. Join author Mike Holliday for a day of sight fishing inshore on the flats where he targets snook, redfish and trout. But on this day his mission will be to cover everything you'll need to see and know to become a successful sight fisherman.

DVD Executive Producer: Cavin Brothers

DVD CHAPTERS:

- ▶ THE APPEAL OF SIGHT FISHING
- ▶ IT'S ALL ABOUT THE EYES
- ▶ TACKLE OPTIONS
- ▶ LOCATING FISH (INSHORE & OFFSHORE)
- ▶ SPOTTING FISH
- ▶ APPROACHING FISH
- ▶ NATURAL BAIT TECHNIQUES
- ▶ ARTIFICIAL BAIT TECHNIQUES
- ▶ READING FISH
- ▶ UNDERSTANDING HOW WEATHER PLAYS A ROLE
- ▶ SIGHT FISHING TECHNIQUES
- ▶ GETTING TALL
- ▶ SIGHT FISHING ON FOOT
  - ▶ PUTTING IT ALL TOGETHER
  - ▶ CONSERVATION

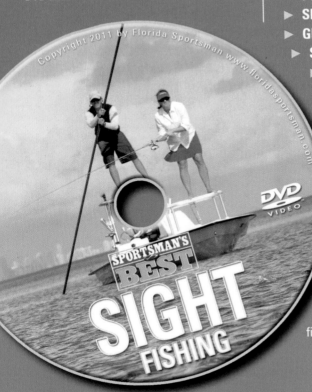

Copyright 2011 by Florida Sportsman www.floridasportsman.com

DVD VIDEO

SPORTSMAN'S BEST SIGHT FISHING

Mike Holliday covers material from the book's chapters, from the Appeal of Sight Fishing all the way to Putting It All Together, brought to life with scenes from seven years of footage from Florida Sportsman TV and Shallow Water Angler TV. No matter where you live, from Texas to Maine, we have something for you. No matter if you're an offshore angler or inshore angler, we've got you covered.

"There's absolutely no better way to experience the excitement of sight fishing than to see it playing out in front of you in HD fish-tailing color."

—*Blair Wickstrom, Publisher, Florida Sportsman*